Inspiring Teens, Tweens, and Families to Make a Difference in the World

Programming to Advance the Sustainable Development Goals

AMANDA MOSS STRUCKMEYER

CHICAGO | 2025

Amanda Moss Struckmeyer holds a master's degree in library and information studies from the University of Wisconsin–Madison and is currently pursuing a doctor of education degree in educational sustainability at the University of Wisconsin–Stevens Point. Having worked in public and school library settings, Amanda has a passion for equity and sustainability. She has served on both the Newbery and Caldecott Award Committees and is the coauthor of *DIY Programming and Book Displays: How to Stretch Your Programming without Stretching Your Budget and Staff* (2010). Amanda lives in Madison, Wisconsin, and works as a library media specialist in an elementary school.

ISBNs
979-8-89255-322-3 (paper)
979-8-89255-318-6 (PDF)

Library of Congress Cataloging-in-Publication Data

Names: Struckmeyer, Amanda Moss, author
Title: Inspiring teens, tweens, and families to make a difference in the world : programming to advance the sustainable development goals / Amanda Moss Struckmeyer.
Description: Chicago : ALA Editions, 2025. | Includes bibliographical references and index.
Identifiers: LCCN 2025012008 (print) | LCCN 2025012009 (ebook) | ISBN 9798892553223 paperback | ISBN 9798892553186 pdf
Subjects: LCSH: Libraries—Activity programs | Sustainable development—Study and teaching | Sustainable Development Goals (Project)—Study and teaching | Libraries and families | Libraries and teenagers | Libraries and children | Children—Political activity | Teenagers—Political activity | Social action—Library resources | BISAC: LANGUAGE ARTS & DISCIPLINES / Library & Information Science / General
Classification: LCC Z716.33 .S77 2025 (print) | LCC Z716.33 (ebook) | DDC 025.5/7338—dc23/eng/20250429
LC record available at https://lccn.loc.gov/2025012008
LC ebook record available at https://lccn.loc.gov/2025012009

Book design by Alejandra Diaz in the FreightText Pro and Effra typefaces.

♾ This paper meets the requirements of ANSI/NISO Z39.48-1992 (Permanence of Paper).

Printed in the United States of America

29 28 27 26 25 5 4 3 2 1

ALA Editions purchases fund advocacy, awareness, and accreditation programs for library professionals worldwide.

CONTENTS

ACKNOWLEDGMENTS

MUCH GRATITUDE TO all who are working, in large and small ways, for social justice, equity, climate solutions, and peace. Many thanks to the Educational Sustainability program at the University of Wisconsin–Stevens Point for allowing me to delve into the topic of sustainability and discover its immeasurable breadth and depth. Dr. Erin Redman, Dr. Cathy Scheder, Dr. Polly Manske, Dr. Lindsay Bernhagen, Dr. Paula DeHart, Dr. Becca Franzen, Dr. Marcus Lewis, Dr. Yue Li, Dr. Rachael Rost-Allen, and Dr. Henry St. Maurice have been instrumental in my progress. Gratitude to Dr. Lara Saguisag, whose guidance and committee membership is appreciated beyond what I can express. To the members of EDSU Cohort 7: future Doctors of Education Kristin Abt, Dani Burhop, Luis Caballero, Angie Foss, Michelle Gullickson, Jennifer Herek, Sara Holtzman, Heidi James, Sarah Kleven, Ashlee Kuhry-Larsen, Tierney Lain, Ana Mendes, Sam Minch, Katherine Riebe, Jared Schroeder, Rachel Tidd, Michelle Titterton, and Jodi Williams, I'm so glad we are in this together. Hugs and love to my daughter, Sophie, who has patiently made time and space for me to work on this book and has always been ready for a game of *Forbidden Island* or a trip to the dog park when I need a distraction.

INTRODUCTION
The Seventeen Sustainable Development Goals

THE SEVENTEEN SUSTAINABLE development goals (SDGs) identified by the United Nations (UN) encompass an ambitious range of issues—world hunger, gender equality, and the climate crisis, to name just a few. These topics may (understandably) feel daunting; we may be at a loss in terms of where to begin our action. That's where this book comes in, offering accessible entry points for discussion and exploration of each goal.

In the following chapters, you'll find ideas and inspiration for book clubs, hands-on STEAM projects, guest speakers, community service opportunities, and much more. These activities are meant to be approachable for librarians and appealing for patrons, and they're easily customizable for different group sizes, programming spaces, budgets, and time frames.

Each of the seventeen programming chapters in this book addresses one sustainable development goal. Of course, there is a considerable amount of overlap between goals, so you'll notice some goals represented in multiple chapters. This is simply the nature of the goals; they're nearly impossible to tease apart completely. You'll also notice that the chapter titles for chapters 1 and 2 use a slight variation from UN's shortened SDG names; the UN uses "No Poverty" and "Zero Hunger" to quickly describe the first two SDGs. In this book, we refer to SDG 1 as "Ending Poverty" and SDG 2 as "Feed the World."

What This Book Is

This book is a collection of programming ideas for tweens, teens, and families, designed to act as springboards for further discovery, discussion, and exploration. By offering programs that incorporate sustainability content, we are part of an effort to normalize conversation around sustainability. This book gives librarians the tools to offer these programs and bring patrons together.

Each chapter includes programming ideas that are perfect for multi-age audiences (families), tweens, and teens. Of course, librarians are creative and resourceful, so please adjust and combine activities in any way that fits your community. The “Passive Programs” sections are full of activities that patrons can engage in at any time. I recommend setting up a passive programming station at your library, so patrons get accustomed to the location of these activities. Passive programming is an excellent way to reach patrons outside of traditional scheduled programs; it offers flexible, cost-effective engagement and can be centered around any topic. At the close of each chapter, a “Community Connections” section offers ideas for partnering up, reaching out, and connecting outside the library’s walls. Guest speakers, outreach opportunities, and other suggestions in these sections encourage librarians to tap into local experts and foster ties among community members.

What This Book Isn’t

This book doesn’t attempt to be all-encompassing, exhaustive, or perfect. There are innumerable ways to engage with and celebrate sustainability; the ideas found in the chapters that follow are just a tiny portion.

Admittedly, some of the activities listed make use of questionably sustainable materials, such as plastic zip-top bags and plastic cups. When possible, reuse these. One set of plastic cups, for example, can be used in many stacking activities. If you’re serving beverages at a program, invite patrons to bring their own water bottles or reusable cups.

My hope is that you’ll find the ideas in this book practical and inspiring, and that the content helps to build your confidence in promoting sustainability through programming.

1 Ending Poverty

Sustainable development goal 1: End poverty in all its forms everywhere.[1]

THE FIRST SUSTAINABLE development goal focuses on eradicating poverty. According to the 2030 Agenda for Sustainable Development, adopted in 2015 at the UN's Sustainable Development Summit, eliminating poverty is the largest global challenge and is absolutely necessary for sustainable development.

Poverty is a complex and multilayered issue. For the purposes of library programming, look for themes within this goal that young people in your community will relate to and understand. Money, entrepreneurship, and overcoming obstacles may be meaningful, accessible, and engaging for tween and teen audiences. The program ideas in this chapter contain elements of these themes.

FAMILY PROGRAMS

Stuff Swap

One great way to save money and make a positive environmental impact is by avoiding purchasing new items when possible. Plan a Stuff Swap, during which patrons of all ages bring intact, usable items and go home with others. As patrons enter, simply have them place their items on tables and then browse and find other items they'd like to take home. Chances are, you'll have lots of leftovers, so be prepared by scheduling a pickup by a local secondhand store. Not ready to take on a full-fledged Stuff Swap? Try a smaller-scale book exchange instead.

Barter and Build

Before this program starts, place a variety of potential building materials in a box. These might include clean, empty food containers, dowels, string, drinking straws, pom-poms, paper, tinfoil, and buttons. Additionally, transform plain index cards into Barter and Build cards by writing a building challenge on each one, such as:

- Something you could wear around your waist
- Something you could drive
- An animal
- Something you could store a book under

During the program, participants take turns choosing items out of the cardboard box (add a challenge by reaching into the box without looking) until each family has a selection of between six and ten items. Next, hand out a Barter and Build card to each family. Tell them that they'll need to build the item on their card with the items they drew from the box (plus tape, which is a bonus item, shared among the entire group). Here's the catch: families can barter and trade items with one another. After participants have had the opportunity to finish trading and building, talk together about why some items were more valuable than others, and how the worth of a certain item changes with its usefulness and scarcity.

Coin Flip Icebreaker, Two Ways

Use a coin as a tool to encourage mingling at the start of any program, or during a transition between activities. Try these two methods:

- Hold a coin in your hands. Ask participants to put their hands on their heads if they believe it will land with the heads side up when you flip it, and to place their hands on their hips if they predict the coin will land tails-up. Flip the coin. Those who guessed correctly remain standing; others sit down. Repeat until one person remains standing.
- Give coins to half of the people in the room. Have them pair up, and ask each set of partners to hold a coin toss. The winner of the coin toss remains in the game, while the other player joins the winner's team by standing behind the winner. Now, winners pair up (with their teams behind them, cheering them on), and when one wins a coin flip, the entire other team joins the winning team. This continues until all players are on one person's team. Be sure to place a container in the center of the room for extra coins as the number of teams dwindles.

Don't Ever Change

Experiment with coins through three STEAM activities.

- Coin Rubbings: Provide a variety of coins (real or artificial; check teaching supply stores for artificial coins), crayons, colored pencils, and paper. Invite participants to lay paper over a coin, then use a crayon or pencil to create a rubbing. If you like, suggest creating pictures, patterns, or designs with the rubbings.
- This Is How We Roll: Challenge participants to roll a coin on its edge. Which type of coin is easiest to roll? Hardest? Which one rolls the farthest? How far is the longest roll? Add elements such as a variety of surfaces (wood, sandpaper, different types of fabric, etc.), and encourage families to build ramps by propping up one end of the rolling surface.
- Weight for Me: Experiment with weighing coins of different denominations. Ask participants to predict the relative weights of the coins by indicating which coin they think is the heaviest and lightest, then ranking the others in between. Use a scale to test their predictions. For an added challenge, have them answer questions such as "How many pennies do you think will weigh the same as two quarters?" or "Which do you think weighs more: fifteen nickels or twenty pennies?" After guessing, have them test their predictions. Add an optional element by experimenting with the weight of a certain monetary value. For example, how much does one dollar weigh in pennies? Nickels? Dimes?

TWEEN PROGRAMS

Book Club: Disaster Strikes!

Natural and human-caused disasters and poverty are a dangerous combination; when a disaster strikes, a community without enough resources to rebuild will face a long-term struggle. Explore this phenomenon with a book club focused on disasters. If you like, choose one disaster as the theme for each meeting, and provide a list of suggested books, including fiction, nonfiction, and graphic novels, for participants to choose from. For example, for a Hurricane Katrina-themed book club meeting, one participant might read *I Survived Hurricane Katrina* by Lauren Tarshis, another might choose the graphic novel version of the same book, while another reads *What Was Hurricane Katrina?* by Robin Koontz. Another might read *Ranger in Time: Hurricane Katrina Rescue* by Kate Messner, and still another might select *Claudia in the Storm: A Hurricane Katrina Survival Story* by Denise Walter McConduit.

Million-Dollar Reads

Host a program centered around the idea of one million dollars, and the number one million in general. Have participants work in small groups to create plans showing what they would do with a million dollars, and talk together about how they came to those decisions and what factors they considered.

Next, experiment with the number one million. Have a kitchen scale, a tape measure, and calculators on hand for conundrums such as:

- How many copies of a particular book would be needed to achieve a weight of one million pounds?
- How many magazines would need to be placed end to end to cover one million miles?
- How many copies of *Harry Potter and the Deathly Hallows* by J. K. Rowling would need to be combined for a total of one million pages?

Discuss or book talk titles such as:

- *Millions* by Frank Cottrell Boyce, an edge-of-your-seat chapter book about two brothers who unexpectedly come into a lot—a *lot*—of cash. They've only got seventeen days to spend it all, but the boys run into trouble when they don't agree on how to use it.
- *The Million Dollar Race* by Matthew Ross Smith, the fictional story of Grant Falloon, who thinks he has a chance at winning a competition for the fastest kid in the world, thereby earning serious prize cash. Inconveniently, Grant doesn't have a birth certificate, so he can't compete for the United States . . . but he can attempt to create a brand-new country of his own in order to qualify for the race.
- *The Get Rich Quick Club* by Dan Gutman, which follows the adventures of Gina Tumolo and her friends, who decide to spend the summer getting rich and generating one million dollars by September. Can they do it?

Book to Movie

Hold a book discussion about *Millions* by Frank Cottrell Boyce (described in the previous section) and then show the movie based on the book.

Toilet Paper Toss Tournament

Book talk or discuss *Death by Toilet Paper* by Donna Gephart, a story about Benjamin, who is determined to generate enough money—quickly—to keep his family from being evicted. When Benjamin notices a toilet paper slogan contest with a hefty cash prize, he's sure this is the golden ticket he's been waiting for.

Set up one or more toilet paper toss stations by cutting a hole in the top of a cardboard box and placing a toilet seat on top. Provide rolls of toilet paper (individually wrapped rolls work well) and facilitate a toilet paper toss tournament.

For additional toilet paper-related fun, create a bocce-inspired game together; challenge players to roll or toss their toilet paper closest to a target on the ground without being knocked out of the way by another player's roll of toilet paper. Encourage the group to generate rules and a scoring system as you play.

TEEN PROGRAMS

Name Your Price

Host your own version of a popular money-related game show, such as *Deal or No Deal* or *The Price Is Right*. If you like, ask teen or adult volunteers to help you create props, configure games, or choose music in preparation for the event.

Teen Entrepreneurs

Invite teens to sign up to sell handmade items at an event at the library. Consider creating a forum at the event for teens to advertise services they offer (such as babysitting or lawn mowing) as well. As a lead-up to the event, hold planning sessions to discuss ideas, and invite local entrepreneurs or business owners to join these sessions to answer questions and offer advice.

Collect $200

Host an afternoon of *Monopoly* games. If you like, provide materials for participants to rebrand a *Monopoly* board into an original version, possibly substituting the names of community landmarks or familiar streets for those on the board. Alternatively, call your program Monopoly Dismantled, and offer old or incomplete copies of the game for teens to use as art supplies. They may wish to make a picture frame out of the *Monopoly* money, a necklace out of one of the houses or place markers (such as the top hat or the car), or a magnet out of one of the Community Chest or Chance cards, for example.

Book Club

Incorporate the books listed here into an existing book club or create a new group. These books, each of which contains a theme related to poverty, provide plenty of fodder for discussion.

- *The Hate U Give* by Angie Thomas
- *Illegal* by Bettina Restrepo
- *In Real Life* by Cory Doctorow and Jen Wang
- *Money Hungry* by Sharon G. Flake
- *Paper Things* by Jennifer Richard Jacobson
- *Smoove City* by Kenny Keil

PASSIVE PROGRAMS

Money Match-Up

Create a matching game for patrons to complete any time they're at the library. Post pictures of currency from around the world, and ask participants to identify where in the world the currency is used. Display books about coins and other currency, such as the DK Eyewitness book *Money* by Joe Cribb, nearby for reference.

Price It!

Invite patrons to participate in an interactive, game show-inspired activity. Try one of these approaches:

- Post a photograph of an item on a bulletin board or wall. This could be something familiar, such as a pencil or a chair, or something less recognized by patrons, such as a high-tech device or a food from another country or region. If you choose something unfamiliar, label the photo with the item's name and function. Challenge participants to respond to the photo by guessing the item's price. Have participants write their answers on sticky notes and add them next to the photo, or write their responses directly on the bulletin board's background paper. After a week, reveal the answer and post a new photograph.

- Add a "then and now" element to this option by inviting participants to guess the cost of the item in a specific year in history, as well as the item's cost today.
- Post photographs of two items; similar to first idea, these could be easily recognizable or unfamiliar. Ask patrons to indicate which item they believe is more expensive by adding a tally mark to a designated area. Add an extra challenge by asking participants to guess the difference in price between the two items. At the end of the week, reveal the items' actual prices and post a new pair of photographs.

Coin Conundrum

Fill a jar or other clear container with coins. Set it at the circulation or reference desk, and invite patrons to make two guesses: the number of coins in the jar, and the total monetary value of the coins in the jar. Provide slips of paper for participants to submit their names and guesses, and at the end of the week or month, announce the answers and the names of the people whose guesses were closest to the answer for each question.

Design It!

Provide paper and a variety of art supplies, and invite patrons to design their own currency. When they're finished, hang it on the wall or a bulletin board. If you like, ask participants to add the title of their currency ("In the United States, we call our money dollars and cents. What do you call the money you designed today?") to their artwork.

COMMUNITY CONNECTIONS

- Organize a donation drive in your library and community. Gather canned goods for the food pantry, outerwear for a shelter or clothing distribution center, or formalwear for teens who may be preparing to attend homecoming or prom.

- If your library offers prizes as part of the summer reading program, create an option for participants to donate their prize. This doesn't cost patrons anything; the library simply donates the money it would have spent on a prize to a charity. Find local, national, or global organizations that your community will be excited about supporting.
- Invite a local economics teacher or professor, or a specialist from a local financial institution, to talk with tweens and teens about economic choices, such as renting vs. leasing a vehicle, investing in the stock market, credit, and compounding interest.

NOTE

1. United Nations, Department of Economic and Social Affairs, Sustainable Development, "Goals, 1," https://sdgs.un.org/goals/goal1.

2

Feed the World

Sustainable development goal 2: End hunger, achieve food security and improved nutrition and promote sustainable agriculture.[1]

BY 2030, OVER 600 million people around the world are projected to face hunger.[2] A growing global population translates into the need for increased sustainability in agriculture, innovation around decreasing food waste, and purposeful access to nutritious food for people living with hunger and malnutrition.[3]

Everyone has the right to safe and healthy food. Explore this sustainable development goal through programs focused on growing, preparing, enjoying, and sharing food. Of course, check with your administrator before serving or sharing food, and ask patrons about food allergies ahead of time.

FAMILY PROGRAMS

Lunchtime! Munch Time!

Share the books *What the World Eats* by Faith D'Aluisio and *What's for Lunch?* by Andrea Curtis. Provide paper plates and art supplies (construction paper, glue, scissors, crayons, markers, withdrawn cookbooks or cooking magazines, and anything else you choose), and invite each participant to create an original meal on his or her plate. Give participants an opportunity to share about what they've created, and observe similarities and differences between their meals.

We All Contribute

Read Oge Mora's *Thank You, Omu!* or any version of the story "Stone Soup." In both stories, community members come together, each contributing a little bit of food, to make something delicious. Replicate this phenomenon by asking each family to bring along a snack to share with the group. Suggest that participants choose easy-to-grasp finger foods. Provide plates and napkins, and talk together about how each family chose their item to bring along. If snacks are not an option, bring a large pot and spoon, and retell "Stone Soup" with props (families will enjoy creating these props during the program or getting creative with simple objects found in your programming space or library).

Andrea Wang Book Club

Share books by Andrea Wang, such as *Watercress*, *Luli and the Language of Tea*, and *Magic Ramen: The Story of Momofuku Ando*, all of which include themes of family, food, culture, and heritage. Talk together about what participants' families eat, and which food traditions have been passed down through generations. Children may be surprised to hear food-related memories from the adults in their lives. If possible, invite participants to bring along a food that reflects their culture or heritage for others to sample.

Community Garden

Share books about gardening or farming, such as *Food for the Future: Sustainable Farms Around the World* by Mia Wenjen or *Down to Earth: How Kids Help Feed the World* by Nikki Tate. Together, plant a community garden. This might be a patch of soil on the library grounds, a raised bed in a corner of the parking lot, or an off-site garden. Depending on your location and climate, plant seeds or seedlings. Provide garden tools and supplies for participants to decorate stakes to identify each type of plant.

TWEEN PROGRAMS

Sweet as Chocolate

Discuss or book talk chocolate-themed books, such as:

- *The Candymakers and the Great Chocolate Chase* by Wendy Mass
- *Charlie and the Chocolate Factory* by Roald Dahl
- *Chocolate Fever* by Robert Kimmel Smith
- *The Chocolate Touch* by Patrick Skene Catling
- *The Whizz Pop Chocolate Shop* by Kate Saunders

Together, share the book *No Monkeys, No Chocolate* by Melissa Stewart and Allen Young, all about the rainforest dwellers who play important roles in the survival of cocoa trees. If you like, enjoy chocolate together with taste tests (try milk, bittersweet, and dark chocolate) or a visit from a local chocolatier.

Pages and Planting

Plan a book discussion or club with a garden theme. Consider books such as *One Time* by Sharon Creech, *Me and Marvin Gardens* by Amy Sarig King, *The Night Garden* by Polly Horvath, and *Seedfolks* by Paul Fleischman. Choose activities related to growing food and other produce: decorate plant pots, tend the community garden, build garden decorations, talk with a local farmer, taste locally grown produce, or plant seeds or seedlings and observe their growth over time.

Food Miles

Display or book talk titles involving farmers' markets, local food, and farming. Show participants a familiar food or beverage, and ask them to guess the number of miles the item traveled from its point of origin (choose foods that are fairly simple to track, such as produce). Then reveal the actual number of miles. Talk together about the impact of a long food journey on the environment.

If you like, format this activity as a group game, awarding a point to the team whose mileage guess is the most accurate for each food. Alternatively, have participants write their individual answers on notecards, keeping their answers hidden until everyone has written a number. Ask them to reveal their answers, then share the actual number of miles. Embed the concept of food miles into a fun, interactive challenge that kids will enjoy and remember.

DIY Sushi

Set up individual sushi stations with seaweed sheets, bamboo rolling mats, rice, and chopped vegetables. Guide participants in creating sushi rolls (alternatively, a local sushi chef may be willing to be a guest teacher during this program). Have soy sauce and pickled ginger on hand for tweens to enjoy their creations right away.

If food preparation isn't an option, or if you'd like to provide an additional sushi-themed activity, offer supplies and instructions for creating sushi from art materials. There are many ways to do this; the Arthurized Home blog has a great tutorial on making sushi with felt.[4] Be sure to provide boxes or plates for the finished sushi.

TEEN PROGRAMS

Build It!

Invite teens, with the help of local craftspeople, woodworkers, woodworking teachers, or other enthusiasts, to build raised planting beds for gardening. Repurpose wooden dresser drawers, barrels, pallets, or other items, giving them new life as raised beds. Send the finished products home with teens, along with instructions on how to fill the beds and a packet or two of raised bed-friendly seeds, or add the beds to the community garden described in the "Family Programs" section in this chapter.

Chef Challenge

Provide a selection of ingredients, and challenge teens to combine any of them to create something edible. This can be a no-cook event (offer ingredients such as olives, carrot sticks, chocolate chips, sliced bread, pickles, and dried fruit) or, if space and resources allow, go big and get kids cooking! If you like, offer a specific category or description as a challenge, such as "Sweet and Snacky" or "Main Dish Mania," or designate a must-use ingredient. Consider inviting local chefs or restaurant owners to advise participants or act as judges.

Recipes, Restaurants, and Reading: A Teen Book Club

Host a teen book club featuring food-themed books, such as:

- *The Music of What Happens* by Bill Konigsberg
- *My Fine Fellow* by Jennieke Cohen
- *The Omnivore's Dilemma: Young Readers Edition* by Michael Pollan
- *A Pho Love Story* by Loan Le
- *The Way You Make Me Feel* by Maurene Goo
- *With the Fire on High* by Elizabeth Acevedo

At your book club meetings, offer an activity or extension project. Try a game show-style challenge centered around food miles (the number of miles a food item travels to reach your area), nutrition, or prices. Try the Peace Corps' food insecurity game, an eye-opener and discussion starter.[5] Or try Global Food Inequality: The Simulation Game from Stairway to SDG, which illustrates the way food is distributed around the world.[6]

Teen Helpers: Hunger in Your Community

Hold this teen volunteer initiative as a one-time or ongoing program. Investigate local food pantries and other organizations that work toward food security for all. Find out whether there are specific needs in your locality, and ask about potential opportunities for teens to assist. Invite personnel from the organizations to visit with teens and answer questions about how their groups function. With teens, decide how they'll contribute. Potential activities for your group might include holding a non-perishable food drive, preparing lunch bags for distribution to unhoused individuals, publicizing food initiatives in the community through posters or online announcements, or even volunteering on-site at food pantries.

PASSIVE PROGRAMS

Recipe Swap

Invite patrons of any age to submit their favorite recipes. Distribute the recipe cards when patrons visit the circulation desk, along with instructions for adding a recipe and returning the card to the library. As cards are returned, post them on a bulletin board or wall, or collect them in a binder (using clear page protectors will make both sides of the cards accessible) for browsing.

Where in the World?

Fill a bulletin board or wall space with pictures of popular foods from around the world. Invite patrons to guess where each food is typically found. Provide an answer key, or create a lift-the-flap-style answer to reveal near each picture. If you like, include each food's name in the language that is commonly spoken in the area where it is found.

Community Garden Upkeep

After planting a community garden (see the family program earlier), invite patrons to contribute to its maintenance any time. Create a list of tasks, such as weeding and watering, that can be done, along with handy information on how to identify a weed and how to know whether the plants need water. As the garden begins to produce vegetables or flowers, make them available for patrons to take home and enjoy.

Little Free Snack Library

In your library's lobby or other common space, create a Little Free Snack Library. This could be as simple as a shelf or two, or even a few plastic milk crates stacked on top of one another, with the open side facing out toward the front. Encourage patrons to drop off shelf-stable snacks and other food items in the Little Free Snack Library, and invite anyone visiting the library to help themselves to the food items. A list of donation guidelines may be helpful for communicating expectations about types of foods, expiration dates, and refrigeration; post this near the Little Free Snack Library and on the library's website.

COMMUNITY CONNECTIONS

- Feature guest speakers or panel members such as chefs, farmers, restauranteurs, and grocery store owners. Discuss sustainability, access issues, food waste, and other topics of interest.
- Host a sustainable food fair. Invite local farms that offer Community Supported Agriculture shares, shop owners whose merchandise is related to sustainable food, farming, or gardening, and other vendors or producers to host tables and share information about their businesses and products. If you're not sure where to start looking for potential vendors and producers, check out a local farmers market. You may find community members selling honey, vegetables, fruit, and baked goods; more importantly, you'll find lots of experts who may be willing to be part of a sustainable food fair.

NOTES

1. United Nations, Department of Economic and Social Affairs, Sustainable Development, "Goals, 2," https://sdgs.un.org/goals/goal2.
2. United Nations, Department of Economic and Social Affairs, Sustainable Development, "Goals, 2."
3. United Nations, Department of Economic and Social Affairs, Sustainable Development, "Food Security and Nutrition and Sustainable Agriculture," https://sdgs.un.org/topics/food-security-and-nutrition-and-sustainable-agriculture.
4. Arthurized Home, "Let's Have a Crafternoon! – Felt Sushi," February 12, 2020, https://arthurizedhome.com/2020/02/12/lets-have-a-crafternoon-felt-sushi/.
5. Peace Corps, "Food Security Game," www.peacecorps.gov/educators-and-students/educators/resources/food-security-game/.
6. Stairway to SDG, "SDG 2—Global Food Inequality, the Simulation Game," https://stairwaytosdg.eu/en/act/144-global-food-inequality-simulation-game#s3.

3

Good Health and Well-Being

Sustainable development goal 3: Ensure healthy lives and promote well-being for all at all ages.[1]

THE THIRD SUSTAINABLE development goal aims at ensuring access to positive physical and mental health for all people. This encompasses medical care at clinics and hospitals, safe roads to prevent accidents, lifestyles and services that contribute to mental health, and disease prevention and treatment.[2] Explore this goal with books and activities related to mindfulness, safety, and healthy bodies.

FAMILY PROGRAMS

Bicycle Bonanza

Invite patrons to learn about bicycle safety and basic maintenance. Bicycle shop personnel and police officers may be available to share information at this event. Display fiction and nonfiction titles about bicycles from your collection. Make the content fun; for example, after learning about hand signals, play a version of Simon Says using cues related to the signals:

- Simon says, "Signal for a right turn."
- Simon says, "Signal for slowing down or stopping."
- Simon says, "Signal for a left turn."

If possible, distribute bicycle lights or reflectors, and provide information on sources for helmets in your area. If space allows, invite patrons to bring their bicycles and ride an obstacle course (set up safety cones or other simple obstacles to maneuver around).

On-the-Go Kits

When families are out and about, unexpected needs often come up. Help them be prepared by hosting an On-the-Go Kit making workshop. Provide containers (or ask patrons to bring them), such as clean rectangular plastic take-out boxes or basic pencil cases (look for these during back-to-school sales). Offer items such as Band-Aids, small flashlights, shelf-stable snacks, and individually wrapped sanitizing wipes, and invite families to choose items to fill their kits. If your budget is limited, consider simply having each family decorate the exterior of a pencil case and send home a list of suggested contents for it. Consider adding a create-a-game element to your program; provide pre-cut cardstock or blank notecards, and have patrons decorate their cards. A memory game, in which participants try to find matching pairs of cards, is fairly easy to create; simply make sets of two cards bearing matching designs and include a short set of instructions to accompany the game. Encourage families to add these games to their kits for on-the-go fun.

Family Yoga

Invite a local yoga teacher to lead a beginner-level class for all ages. If waivers are required, be sure to have them available before class. Display yoga-themed books for patrons to peruse after this program.

Obstacle Course

Enjoy physical movement with an obstacle course. Set up a course in your programming space, in the library's common area, or outdoors using hula hoops, painters' tape, playground balls, and other supplies. Tweens and teens may enjoy helping to design and set up the course. Some challenges along the course could include:

- Jumping into a hoop, then back out
- Bouncing a ball three times
- Tiptoe walking along a line of painters' tape

Books to accompany this program could include *Skater Cielo* by Rachel Katstaller, *Hop, Hop, Jump!* by Lauren Thompson, and *Explorers of the Wild* by Cale Atkinson.

TWEEN PROGRAMS

Breathe In . . . Breathe Out

Explore mindful breathing techniques with books such as *Just Breathe: Meditation, Mindfulness, Movement, and More* by Mallika Chopra and *Mindfulness for Kids in 10 Minutes a Day: Simple Exercises to Feel Calm, Focused, and Happy* by Maura Bradley. Together, try some of the techniques. Create posters that include illustrations and instructions on specific techniques, and hang these around the library to encourage all library visitors to engage in mindful breathing.

Riddle Me This Book Club

Brain-teasers and other puzzles are great for exercising our brains. Host a tween book club centered on books involving riddles, scavenger hunts, and unlikely solutions. At each meeting, share a few brain-teasers or riddles. Choose books such as:

- *Escape from Mr. Lemoncello's Library* series by Chris Grabenstein
- *The Mysterious Benedict Society* series by Trenton Lee Stewart
- *The Parker Inheritance* by Varian Johnson
- *The Westing Game* by Ellen Raskin

Sports Inventors

Give tweens the chance to invent their own sports. Provide playground balls, hula hoops, badminton racquets, and other supplies for games and sports. Bring books such as *Weird but True! Sports* by National Geographic or the DK Eyewitness book *Sports* by Tim Hammond for browsing and sharing. Working in small groups, have patrons determine the rules, supplies, scoring system, and playing area for their new sports. Then have groups teach one another their games and try them out.

Laugh a Little

Laughing is good for you.[3] Pull books of jokes and riddles from your collection to share at this event. Have a few jokes ready to start the program, and then give participants time to peruse the books, find their favorite jokes, and share them with the group. If you like, take videos of tweens telling jokes, and post these on your library's website or social media pages.

TEEN PROGRAMS

Basic First Aid and CPR

Host a first aid and/or CPR training by the American Red Cross or your local fire department or emergency response organization. If you plan to offer certification, be sure to ask about the requirements, and clearly communicate these to teens and their caregivers. If holding a training isn't a good fit for your library, host a panel of emergency personnel, who can answer questions about their jobs, training, and equipment.

Escape Room Challenge

Just as we exercise our bodies, challenging our minds is part of staying healthy, too. Create an original escape room with a series of questions, riddles, physical challenges, and puzzles, with each one's answer leading teens to the next challenge. If time is tight, consider purchasing an escape room kit, complete with everything you'll need for a memorable event. During the escape room program, display teen mystery books.

Mini Golf Course Creation

Provide cardboard, duct tape, paint, construction paper, plastic cups, and other materials for teens to use to create miniature golf course holes. After all the holes are finished, try them out. Then set them up around the library for patrons to enjoy any time (see the "Tee Up!" game in the "Passive Programs" section).

Move It! Book Club

For teens who like to try new physical activities, host a book club focused on movement. A one-time event might include several book talks and opportunities for participants to sample a few activities. Alternatively, an ongoing club could include a discussion of one title that participants read in advance and a more in-depth experience with the related physical movement. Inviting a community expert, such as a fitness instructor, coach, or dance teacher, may be beneficial. Try these books and activities:

- *Can't Stop Won't Stop: A Hip-Hop History* (Young Adult Edition) by Jeff Chang and Dave "Davey D" Cook: Try some hip-hop dance moves after discussing this nonfiction title.

- *Eleanor & Park* by Rainbow Rowell: This story is set in the 1980s; try pairing it with step aerobics, which was popular during that time.
- *Rez Ball* by Byron Graves: Shoot some hoops or practice dribbling or passing to accompany this basketball-centered story.

PASSIVE PROGRAMS

Road Rules Quiz

Post questions about driving rules on a bulletin board or wall, and invite patrons to guess at the answers. Post pictures of road signs and ask what they signify, or base your quiz on driving rules for your state or area. Add lift-the-flap features to reveal the answers.

Take a Breath

Create and hang mindfulness technique posters around the library, encouraging patrons to pause and breathe. If you like, enlist the help of tween volunteers to create these posters, highlighting various breathing techniques.

Anatomy Experts

Create a handout listing medical terms for body parts, along with common terminology, and ask participants to connect the matching words. Try terms such as:

- Cranium (head)
- Mentis (chin)
- Hallux (big toe)
- Axilla (armpit)

Tee Up!

Set up miniature golf holes created by teens (see the teen program "Mini Golf Course Creation" in this chapter) around the library. Offer lightweight plastic golf clubs and golf balls at the circulation or reference desk, and encourage patrons to try their hands at miniature golf. Mini golf at the library makes a great after-hours event, too.

COMMUNITY CONNECTIONS

- Invite guest speakers such as nutritionists, doctors, and fitness instructors who can offer high-interest material and a connection to local services.
- Locate a recreational race (such as a 5K) in your area, and organize a library team to run and/or walk together. Offer a few optional training sessions leading up to the event. In addition, matching shirts or sweatbands are a fun, community-building touch.

NOTES

1. United Nations, Department of Economic and Social Affairs, Sustainable Development, "Goals, 3," https://sdgs.un.org/goals/goal3.
2. United Nations, Sustainable Development Goals, "Goal 3 – Good Health and Well-Being Reading List," www.un.org/sustainabledevelopment/sdgbookclub/3archive/.
3. Mayo Clinic, "Healthy Lifestyle, Stress Management," www.mayoclinic.org/healthy-lifestyle/stress-management/in-depth/stress-relief/art-20044456.

4
Quality Education

Sustainable development goal 4: Ensure inclusive and equitable quality education and promote lifelong learning opportunities for all.[1]

DESPITE PROGRESS IN increasing access to education, 57 million primary school-aged children are still not in school. Dangerous commutes to school, financial burdens, lack of qualified teachers, and lack of safe school buildings contribute to this problem.[2]

Education is important in and of itself, but it also opens doors to achieving other sustainable development goals. Individuals who are educated are more likely to find well-paying jobs and stay out of poverty. Educated people are more likely to make healthy choices regarding diet, exercise, and other lifestyle factors. And when education is available for all, the gender divide decreases.

Explore this sustainable development goal through stories and activities centered on the themes of school, learning, and education. Keep in mind that education can take many different forms, such as homeschooling, online or distance learning, public school, and private school. Consider hosting these programs in August, when families are preparing for children to begin a new school year.

FAMILY PROGRAMS

I Spy School Jars

Gather a variety of small school-related items, such as erasers, crayons, magnetic letters and numbers, and dice. Provide clear plastic jars (or ask patrons to bring them along), and guide participants in creating I Spy jars. Simply fill the jar with sand, small rocks, or beads, adding the school-related objects throughout the filling process. Leave some space at the top of the jar so that the contents can move around easily. Encourage families to play I Spy using their jars. For example, a caregiver can give a clue for an item they want the child to find in the jar, such as, “I spy something green.” The child then searches and guesses until they name the correct item. Clue givers can give additional clues as needed. Children will love taking turns giving clues to their caregivers or other participants in the event. If you like, create one jar to use as part of a passive program, as described later in this chapter.

We Are All Teachers

Encourage patrons to share what they know at this program. Ask families to bring something to teach other attendees; this could be a song, a fact, a simple art activity, a game, or even a recipe. Have families take turns teaching one another. If you like, create a written collection of materials that were shared at the program. Keep a printed copy in the library for browsing, and distribute digital copies to all participants.

Whose Story Is It?

Share the book *School’s First Day of School* by Adam Rex, in which a new school building is nervous about the first day of class. The school itself is the main character of the story. Invite participants to brainstorm together about other items that could be main characters—perhaps pencils that are excited to be used to write stories, or books that are hoping to be checked out of the library. In small groups, have patrons create written stories or short skits or puppet shows, featuring an object as the central character. During this program, also consider sharing *The Crayons Go Back to School* by Drew Daywalt, about a group of crayons and the subjects they’re looking forward to as a new school year begins.

I ♥ My Teacher

Host a thank-you note writing event, during which participants create cards or stationery and write to teachers who have made an impact on their lives. Provide a variety of paper, envelopes, art supplies, and writing utensils. If you like, offer to deliver the notes to local schools or mail them to institutions further away. Add a technology element by creating a collection of brief videos featuring patrons (and library staff) expressing their thanks and gratitude toward teachers. Host this on your library’s social media page or on a video-sharing site, such as Flip.

TWEEN PROGRAMS

Building Innovation

Around the world, students travel to school using a variety of modes of transportation. Share excerpts from the book *Off to Class: Incredible and Unusual Schools Around the World* by Susan Hughes, which features photographs and detailed information about schools in the desert, in the rainforest, and even on a boat. Many of these schools were created in response to specific environmental challenges, such as floods, hurricanes, and earthquakes. Next, challenge participants, individually or in teams, to build models of schools using any building materials you choose to provide—these could include Lego bricks, plastic cups, sheets of paper, fabric, cardboard boxes, empty plastic bottles, and more. Give builders a set of criteria, including such requirements as "Your school must have an entrance for students" or "Your school must have at least two rooms." Also give each builder or team a challenge they'll need to accommodate in their design. Challenges might include:

- Your city floods often.
- Your school has no running water.
- Your community is located in a very hot area.

For an added twist, present the challenge cards fifteen minutes after builders have begun their work. They'll need to adjust their plans and make some changes! As participants finish building, ask them to share their designs and the strategies they used to work with the challenges.

Graphic Novel Book Club

Host a book club focused on school-related graphic novels. Offer the novels profiled in the following sections as a series of programs, or choose a single program to host as a stand-alone event.

In the Halls of Middle School

Discuss Jerry Craft's *New Kid*, *Class Act*, and *School Trip*, all featuring middle school characters dealing with real-life struggles. Online, you'll find video tutorials by Jerry Craft; show these to the group and invite participants to draw the characters from the books. For adventurous artists, watch Shelf Stuff's *Blindfold Drawing Challenge* video featuring Jerry Craft, and take a stab at drawing a character with closed eyes or a blindfold.[3]

On the Wild Side

The *Mr. Wolf's Class* series by Aron Nels Steinke is full of outrageous high jinks that readers might expect from a fourth-grade class full of animals. Follow the discussion with a rousing game of "What Time Is It, Mr. Wolf?" All players begin behind a starting line, aside from one player ("Mr. Wolf") who begins at the other end of the playing area, behind a finish line. Mr. Wolf faces away from the players, who ask him, "What time is it, Mr. Wolf?" His response dictates the number of steps forward players may take. For example, if he says, "It's seven o'clock," all players move forward seven steps. Mr. Wolf may also choose to say, "It's lunchtime!" while turning around and chasing after the rest of the players, who attempt to return to the starting area without being tagged. If Mr. Wolf tags someone, that player becomes the new Mr. Wolf.

Monster Readers

For science fiction fans, try *Monster Mayhem* by Christopher Eliopoulos. Readers will meet brilliant young Zoe, whose advanced robotics skills earn her a place at a special technology school. Zoe loves the monsters she sees in the movies, but she knows they're fantastical . . . until one shows up in her yard. Follow this discussion with a hands-on robotics activity, such as building bristle bots (find instructions at PBS Kids online).[4]

Splish, Splash

Swim Team by Johnnie Christmas follows Bree, who is excited to start at a new middle school—but she's not so excited about the swimming elective in her schedule. If time and space allow, host a water balloon toss, or create an obstacle course using pool noodles (find inspiration at PBS Kids online).[5]

TEEN PROGRAMS

Test Your Knowledge

Book talk, display, or discuss books from your collection related to school and education. Play a *Jeopardy*-inspired game in which all of the questions and answers are about the local high school, well-known teachers in the community, and schools in general (for example, "This unstructured time is often spent outdoors, on a playground").

Take a Stand!

Discuss thought-provoking books, such as *I Am Malala* by Malala Yousafzai, a memoir available in adult young readers' editions, and *The Assignment* by Liza Wiemer, a novel based on a true story about two high school seniors who are tasked with arguing in support of the Nazis. Talk together about why some of the issues in the books evoke strong emotions and reactions, and what we can do to create change in the world. Ask a local city council member or other government official to attend as a special guest and discuss change processes and how teens can have their voices heard.

Truth or Lie?

Discuss *One of Us Is Lying* by Karen M. McManus, a mystery thriller featuring five high school students who end up in detention together. The catch: only four students leave detention alive that day, and all four of them immediately become suspects in the fifth student's murder. The first in a three-book series, this volume includes plenty of fodder for discussion and analysis. If you like, expand this into a three-part book club, and meet once per title in the series. Begin or end your program with the game Two Truths and a Lie. Have one person share three facts about themselves: two that are true and one that isn't. The rest of the group must guess which facts are true and which is the lie.

Teen Leaders

Give teens an opportunity to play a leading role in education for younger students. Connect with local preschool or elementary teachers and ask if they have tasks teens could help with. This might include preparing materials (cutting shapes from paper or felt, for example) or recording videos with positive messages, greetings, or (with publisher permission) read-alouds. If creativity and interest allow, consider writing original scripts, creating puppets, and recording a puppet show that aligns with themes teachers are covering in their classes. Writing encouraging notes to older elementary students, especially just before state tests, can also be impactful.

PASSIVE PROGRAMS

Roll Call

Challenge patrons to name the schools attended or staffed by fictional characters. Create a handout with a list of characters; provide spaces for participants to write the name of the corresponding schools. Alternatively, include two lists in your handout: one list of characters, and one list of schools. Ask patrons to match each character with one of the schools by drawing a line between them. Consider including the following characters and schools:

- Harry Potter (Hogwarts School of Witchcraft and Wizardry)
- Anne Shirley (Queen's Academy)
- Mrs. Jewls and Mrs. Gorf (Wayside School)
- Ms. Frizzle (Walkerville Elementary School)
- Greg Heffley (Larry Mack Junior Middle School)
- Auggie Pullman (Beecher Preparatory School)
- Bella Swan (Forks High School)
- Kristy Thomas (Stoneybrook Middle School)

School Scramble

Post an education-related word or phrase on a wall or bulletin board, and challenge participants to create as many words as possible using the letters in that word or phrase. For example, you might post the phrase "Education Is Power." Words that could be created using these letters include:

- Pie
- Wipe
- Date
- Row
- Doctor
- Action

If you like, invite participants to submit their word lists and contact information, and draw a random response to designate a prize winner. Change the word or phrase each week to keep library visitors engaged.

I Spy Challenge

Using the school-themed "I Spy" jar created in the family program earlier in this chapter, hold a challenge for patrons to complete any time they're at the library. Create a list of items you've hidden in the jar, and ask participants to find each one. Alternatively, have patrons list each item they see in the jar. Keep an answer key at the circulation or reference desk that visitors can use to check their responses.

Get on the Bus!

On a wall or bulletin board, post a large paper school bus. Invite patrons to stop at the circulation or reference desk, where a staff member will take instant-print photos of them. Provide scissors and tape so that community members can trim their photos (removing any background) and add them to the bus, situating them to look like they're riding the bus. If your library hosts a reading incentive program, consider offering this activity as a milestone when the program is completed or when a certain goal is met.

COMMUNITY CONNECTIONS

- Invite teachers of all types to share about their careers. Reach out to elementary, secondary, higher education, nontraditional, and other teachers in your area to join an expert panel on teaching.
- Reach out to your local school district to find out about back-to-school events and other functions, such as sports games and family nights. Inquire about hosting a table at these events to share information about upcoming library programs, new books, and more. Consider bringing a giveaway or a simple make-and-take activity, such as a bookmark, so that patrons have a memento to remind them of the library.

NOTES

1. United Nations, Department of Economic and Social Affairs, Sustainable Development, "Goals, 4," https://sdgs.un.org/goals/goal4.
2. Global Campaign for Education, "Results Educational Fund, Global," https://www.gce-us.org/results-educational-fund.
3. YouTube, "Blindfold Drawing Challenge ft. Jerry Craft, New Kid," February 11, 2019, https://youtu.be/DluRrU1Lp6k?si=dyNaWSv7wtNfUAHg.
4. PBS Kids Global, Design Squad Global, Build, "Bristle Bots," https://pbskids.org/designsquad/build/bristle-bots/.
5. PBS Kids for Parents, "Pool Noodle Obstacle Course," September 18, 2019, www.pbs.org/parents/crafts-and-experiments/pool-noodle-obstacle-course.

5 Gender Equality

Sustainable development goal 5: Achieve gender equality and empower all women and girls.[1]

AROUND THE WORLD, women and girls face discrimination, violence, and inequality. Closing the pay gap, ensuring that girls and women have access to education and health care, and eliminating violence and early forced marriage are among the main focus points of goal 5.

Gender can be a sensitive subject; this is an excellent opportunity to model inclusivity. While this goal simply uses the terms "women" and "girls," the International Lesbian, Gay, Bisexual, Trans, and Intersex Association reminds us that these terms include lesbian, bisexual, and transgender individuals.

Explore this sustainable development goal with books and activities that celebrate and affirm women and girls around the world—and in your own community.

FAMILY PROGRAMS

A Is for Ambitious

Share Meena Harris's books, *Ambitious Girl* and *A Is for Ambitious*, which challenge the labels often put on women and girls, such as "loud" and "bossy." Invite participants to think and talk about the qualities that make them strong and unique. Provide paper and art supplies for patrons to create one-page works of art inspired by *A Is for Ambitious*. One approach might include drawing or painting a large letter on the paper, then writing an accompanying statement and filling the rest of the page with a corresponding illustration. For example, a participant might draw a large letter C on her paper, then write, "C is for courageous. I'm courageous when I try new things." The illustration might show the artist jumping into the deep end of a pool or standing at the door of a new school. Send completed projects home with patrons or bind them into a book for browsing at the library.

Speak Out and Speak Up!

Celebrate the power of voice with books such as *Sharice's Big Voice: A Native Kid Becomes a Congresswoman* by Sharice Davids with Nancy K. Mays, and *Speak Up* by Miranda Paul, both of which inspire readers to use their voices to speak out about what is right. Follow these books with a make-a-megaphone art activity. Ahead of time, print a megaphone template, such as the one found on the Activity Author's website,[2] on white cardstock. Provide scissors, glue or tape, and art supplies. Guide participants in decorating and assembling their megaphones. Try them out by having patrons speak at a normal talking volume without the megaphone, and then with the megaphone. If you like, provide a decibel meter to measure the difference in volume.

Fly High

Share the book *Fly, Girl, Fly! Shaesta Waiz Soars Around the World* by Nancy Roe Pimm, a picture book biography about a refugee from Afghanistan who faces gender stereotypes as she overcomes obstacle after obstacle on the way to achieving her dream of becoming a pilot. At age thirty, Shaesta became the youngest woman—and the first from Afghanistan—to circumnavigate the globe solo in a single-engine aircraft.

Together, create straw gliders. Participants may be skeptical that these creations will fly; this is part of the beauty of this project. Each person will need one standard drinking straw, one index card (3 inches × 5 inches), scissors, tape, a ruler, and a pencil. Using the pencil and ruler, draw two lines on the index card, creating three columns, each one inch wide. Cut down the lines; this yields three strips of paper. Tape two of the strips together, slightly overlapping the short ends by about half an inch and taping them together. Now bring the untaped ends of these strips together, creating a hoop. Again, overlap the ends and tape into place. Set this large hoop aside, and create a smaller hoop by taping the short ends of the remaining strip of index card to one another, overlapping the ends slightly. This gives you two paper hoops. Set the straw on the table. Under one end, slide one side of the big hoop. Under the other end, slide one side of the small hoop. Tape the straw to the hoops. You've created a straw glider! Try tossing it (small end first) and see what happens. Experiment with moving the hoops slightly to different parts of the straw.

Learn with Malala

Pakistani education activist Malala Yousafzai has worked tirelessly for girls to have access to education. Books on Yousafzai span all levels, from board books to adult biographies. For a multi-age group, try a read-aloud such as *Malala's Magic Pencil* by Malala Yousafzai. Facilitate a discussion in which participants identify characteristics they share with Malala. Present each person at the program with a pencil (consider purchasing unique pencils ahead of time). Ask individuals or families to draw what they wish for, like Malala hoped to do with her magic pencil. If you like, ask participants to share about what they drew.

TWEEN PROGRAMS

Rebel Girls Book Club

Choose a collection of short biographies about women, such as the *Rebel Girls* series by various authors or *Women Who Dared* by Linda Skeers. Each time your book club meets, focus on a specific individual. Encourage participants to learn about this person in advance of the club meeting; provide recommendations for print and online sources, such as short videos or articles found via the library's databases. During the meeting, discuss the woman, and if you like, read aloud from the biography collection. Include a hands-on activity that corresponds with the subject.

The following programs can be held as four parts of the Rebel Girls Book Club, or they can be offered independently as stand-alone programs.

Cast Your Vote

Celebrate Stacey Abrams (featured in *Rebel Girls Lead: 25 Tales of Powerful Women*) and others who have fought for women's right to vote. Share material from your library collection, and introduce *Citizen She! The Global Campaign for Women's Voting Rights* by Caroline Stevan and Elina Braslina, a graphic novel about women's fight for the right to vote throughout history and around the world. After discussing the book, set out several types of snacks and ask participants to vote for the one they think is best. Before voting, though, ask if the group thinks that everyone should have a vote. Why or why not? Who gets to vote, and who gets to determine this? This may lead to a lively discussion about equal rights at the polls.

It's Your Serve

Explore tennis greats Venus and Serena Williams (featured in *Rebel Girls Champions: 25 Tales of Unstoppable Athletes*). Share a short biography, such as *Game Changers: The Story of Venus and Serena Williams* by Lesa Cline-Ransome, or *Sisters and Champions: The True Story of Venus and Serena Williams* by Howard Bryant. Hold a table tennis tournament or, if resources allow, try full-fledged tennis.

Be Notorious

Supreme Court Justice Ruth Bader Ginsburg (featured in *Rebel Girls Lead: 25 Tales of Powerful Women*) wore distinct collars with her robe to express her feelings toward other Supreme Court members' actions. Share about Ginsburg's legacy of working for gender equality and women's rights. Read aloud *I Dissent: Ruth Bader Ginsburg Makes Her Mark* by Debbie Levy, and invite participants to create original RBG-style collars using the reproducible pattern found on the Explore Children's Museum website.[3]

Put Pen to Paper

Poet Amanda Gorman (featured in *Rebel Girls Celebrate Neurodiversity: 25 Tales of Creative Thinkers*) has overcome obstacles and inspired people around the world with her poetry. Highlight her work, including *Change Sings* and *Something, Someday*, picture books by Amanda Gorman that are likely in your library collection. Invite participants to write their own poetry in any style (visit the poetry section for inspiration) or read poems aloud that they enjoy.

TEEN PROGRAMS

Fly Like a Girl

Celebrate women in aviation—a field traditionally dominated by men. Share selections from *Fly Girls: How Five Daring Women Defied All Odds and Made Aviation History* (Young Readers' Edition) by Keith O'Brien, and *Women Aviators: 26 Stories of Pioneer Flights, Daring Missions, and Record-Setting Journeys* by Karen Gibson. Follow this with a paper airplane challenge. Provide a variety of paper styles and weights, along with books on folding paper airplanes. Challenge participants to build an airplane that will fly the furthest, the highest, or do a loop-the-loop. Encourage teens to work together and build on one another's ideas.

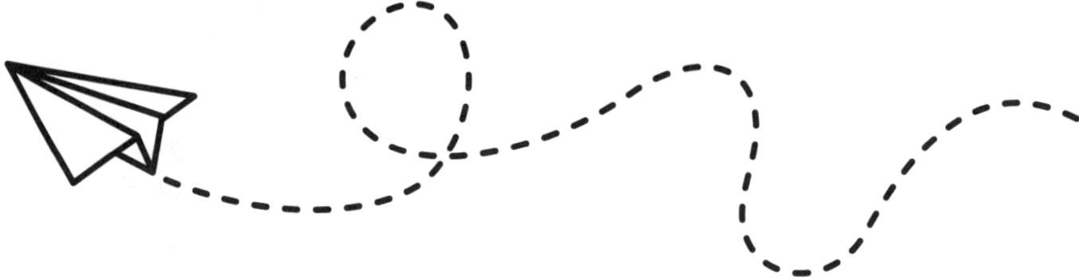

Read and Watch

Host a book discussion and movie-viewing party. Ahead of time, ask participants to read *Hidden Figures: The American Dream and the Untold Story of the Black Women Mathematicians Who Helped Win the Space Race* by Margot Lee Shetterly in the original or young readers' edition. During the program, discuss the book and watch the 2016 film, *Hidden Figures*. Talk about the differences between the book and the movie and the main takeaways from either one.

Girl Power Podcast

Create a forum for teens to share their book recommendations and personal reflections. Invite teens to record an interview about a specific book, including a brief summary of it, an explanation of the book's strengths and potential audience, and any personal connections or inspirations prompted by reading it. Edit and post the recording as a podcast on your library website or a podcasting platform. Choose titles to recommend from your collection; consider these possibilities:

- *Drawn That Way* by Elissa Sussman tells the story of seventeen-year-old Hayley Saffitz, who is determined to make it as an animation director. The opportunity of a lifetime comes along when Hayley snags a spot in her idol's summer program, and Hayley aims to get one of the program's few directing opportunities. The catch: all of the director positions go to boys. Readers will cheer Hayley on as she navigates the lopsided system and remains focused on her goals.
- *Moxie* by Jennifer Mathieu is set in small-town Texas, where sixteen-year-old Viv is sick and tired of sexism, harassment, and the infallibility of the football team. Through anonymous zines, she surprises herself by spurring a feminist revolution.
- *Smash the Patriarchy: A Graphic Novel* by Marta Breen and Jenny Jordahl, an award-winning look at the history of patriarchal systems and an inspiring call to dismantle them. Note that this highly recommended book does contain nudity.

Sing It!

Host a karaoke party, featuring songs by female singers and songwriters. Look for tracks by Taylor Swift, Lady Gaga, Beyoncé, Aretha Franklin, and others. If teens are shy about singing solo, try group karaoke, or project music videos on a big screen and sing along. Alternatively, look for a local piano player who will share their skills by hosting a play-and-sing (similar to the piano bar experience, without the bar).

Take this program to the next level by including thematic, interactive snacks. For example, invite participants to make their own "Shake It Off" pretzels by dipping large pretzel sticks in melted chocolate, then shaking sprinkles in a variety of color choices on top.

PASSIVE PROGRAMS

Name That Hero

Post noteworthy accomplishments by girls and women, and encourage patrons to identify the corresponding individuals. This could take place online via your library's social media channels or website, or in person on a bulletin board. Post one accomplishment per day, or post them all at once. Post the answers under a lift-the-flap-style folded sheet of paper on the bulletin board, or have patrons submit guesses and receive the correct answers at the circulation or reference desk. If you're hosting this activity online, wait for comments or guesses to be submitted, then reveal the answer, along with a link to a video of or about the individual. Ask your teen advisory board, if available, to find content for this program. A few ideas to start with:

- As a girl, she had polio. A doctor told her she might never walk again. She went on to become an Olympic gold medalist in track and field. (Wilma Rudolph)
- At age fifteen, she became a climate activist. She was nominated for a Nobel Peace Prize in 2019, and she started the global Fridays for the Future movement. (Greta Thunberg)
- She is the only scientist to have won two Nobel prizes. (Marie Curie)
- She was the first elected female Muslim prime minister of an Islamic country (Pakistan, from 1988 to 1990 and 1993 to 1996). (Benazir Bhutto)

Women's History Timeline

Create a timeline on the wall of the library; hang up butcher paper, draw a long line, and mark years or decades, depending on the scope of your timeline (you may wish to go way back, or you might choose to stay more current and focus on events in the past fifty or one hundred years). Provide informational books on women's history, along with writing utensils near the timeline. Post QR codes near this program station, leading to related online resources such as the Women's Rights Timeline from the National Archives,[4] which includes primary source photographs and documents, or the interactive global timeline from UN Women.[5] Encourage patrons to use the books and online resources to find accomplishments or breakthroughs for women and girls and add them to the timeline.

Community Thank-You Notes

Create a bulletin board featuring photos of local women and girls who are doing great things. These may be firefighters, EMTs, police officers, doctors, government officials, teachers, business owners, innovators such as high school club leaders, and others. Label each photograph with the individual's first name and a brief description of what she does to help the community. Provide blank cards and art supplies, and invite patrons to decorate and write a thank-you note to one or more of the featured community members. Collect the completed cards at the reference or circulation desk, and at the close of the program, send the cards to the appropriate people.

Say What?!

Participants of all ages will enjoy completing feminist quotes. Provide handouts with the following quotes (or choose others), replacing a word with a blank space in each one. Challenge patrons to fill in the blanks to complete the quotes. If you like, include a word bank and an answer key at the bottom of the page.

- "A woman needs a man like a fish needs a bicycle." —Irina Dunn
- "If they don't give you a seat at the table, bring a folding chair." —Shirley Chisholm
- "I figure, if a girl wants to be a legend, she should go ahead and be one." —Calamity Jane
- "Human rights are women's rights, and women's rights are human rights." —Hillary Clinton
- "We cannot all succeed when half of us are held back." —Malala Yousafzai
- "Women have always been the strong ones of the world." —Coco Chanel
- "A woman with a voice is, by definition, a strong woman." —Melinda Gates
- "There is no limit to what we, as women, can accomplish." —Michelle Obama
- "Each time a woman stands up for herself, without knowing it possibly, without claiming it, she stands up for all women." —Maya Angelou
- "I do not wish women to have power over men; but over themselves." —Mary Shelley
- "We need to reshape our own perception of how we view ourselves. We have to step up as women and take the lead." —Beyoncé

- "I want all the girls without an exception to have that space for themselves where they have opportunities to be the women they wish to be." —Priyanka Chopra
- "Women have discovered that they cannot rely on men's chivalry to give them justice." —Helen Keller
- "In the future, there will be no female leaders. There will just be leaders." —Sheryl Sandberg
- "Think like a queen. A queen is not afraid to fail. Failure is another stepping-stone to greatness." —Oprah Winfrey
- "My hope for the future, not just in the music industry, but in every young girl I meet, is that they all realize their worth and ask for it." —Taylor Swift
- "It's important to teach our female youth that it's OK to say, 'Yes, I am good at this,' and you don't hold back." —Simone Biles
- "Our collective experience has shown that when women have the power to make their own choices, good things happen." —Madeleine Albright
- "Above all, be the heroine of your life, not the victim." —Nora Ephron
- "Women belong in all places where decisions are being made. It shouldn't be that women are the exception." —Ruth Bader Ginsburg
- "Every woman's success should be an inspiration to another. We're strongest when we cheer each other on." —Serena Williams

COMMUNITY CONNECTIONS

- Invite a local female musician or band to perform at the library. Hold a meet-and-greet event before or after the show to foster conversation between the musicians and audience members.
- Hang works of art by local female artists in the library for display. If you like, add reproductions of works by women artists throughout history, such as Frida Kahlo, Georgia O'Keeffe, Maira Kalman, and Yayoi Kusama.
- Host a series of high-interest female speakers. Contact a local university or college, sports team, business bureau, zoo, or other community organization to seek out potential guests. Patrons of all ages may be interested in hearing from an entomologist, a mayor, a chef, an engineer, a farmer, an athlete, and more. If community member availability is limited, contact individuals outside your area and invite them to join a program as a presenter or panel member via videoconferencing software.

- Invite local women-owned businesses to showcase their work at a Meet the Owner fair. Provide a table for each business, and encourage owners to bring materials, handouts, samples, or hands-on opportunities for patrons to engage with their products, services, or other work. This is a chance for community members to meet the women behind familiar local companies, and it's also a venue for businesses to share more about themselves.

NOTES

1. United Nations, Department of Economic and Social Affairs, Sustainable Development, "Goals, 5," https://sdgs.un.org/goals/goal5.
2. Activity Author, "Art Templates," https://activityauthor.com/art-templates/.
3. Explore! Children's Museum, "Ruth Bader Ginsburg Collar Design," www.exploremuseum.org/sandbox-activity/ruth-bader-ginsburg-collar-design.
4. National Archives, Women's Rights, "Women's Rights Timeline," www.archives.gov/women/timeline.
5. UN Women, "Women's Footprint in History," https://interactive.unwomen.org/multimedia/timeline/womensfootprintinhistory/en/index.html.

6 Clean Water and Sanitation

Sustainable development goal 6: Ensure availability and sustainable management of water and sanitation for all.[1]

THE MOST BASIC of human needs, access to water and sanitation is necessary for health, well-being, and life itself. Our bodies are made up of around 60 percent water. We rely on clean water for cooking, drinking, and keeping ourselves and our surroundings clean. Agriculture, industry, and the generation of power all hinge on the availability of water.

Despite the essential nature of water, this resource is limited, and access to water is inconsistent across the globe. According to the United Nations, in 2016, two out of every five health care facilities in the world lacked soap and water (and alcohol-based hand rub), and in 2017, billions of people lacked access to safely managed drinking water.[2] A growing population, rising temperatures, and pollution all threaten Earth's limited water supply.

Explore this sustainable development goal by sharing books and activities centered around water, the roles water plays, sustainable water practices, and more.

FAMILY PROGRAMS

Suncatchers

There's nothing like a drink of water on a hot, sunny day. Share the book *A Cool Drink of Water* by Barbara Kerley, which features stunning photographs from around the world of people collecting and drinking water. Draw on a paper coffee filter with washable markers, leaving some space empty. Spray or gently pour a small amount of water onto the filter. Watch as the water carries the ink, creating a new, unique look. When the filter dries, use it as a suncatcher and hang it on or near a window to catch the sun's rays, so they disperse into a room.

Measuring Rain

Introduce the book *Hope Springs* by Eric Walters, based on true events during a drought in Mbooni District, Kenya. Local villagers refused water to children at the local orphanage, and young Boniface comes up with an idea that not only brings water to the village but also forges understanding between residents.

To measure rainfall in your neighborhood, cut all the way around a clean, empty plastic bottle (such as a discarded soda or water bottle) of any size near the top, just below the spot where the bottle begins to get smaller, eventually getting small enough for the cap. In the base of the bottle, place a small handful of stones or gravel. Add enough water to cover the gravel or stones. Using a fine-tipped permanent marker and a ruler, make a small horizontal line at the level of the water, and label this line as zero (0). Measure up the side of the bottle, marking every quarter inch and labeling every inch. With the cap removed, invert the top of the bottle (the part you cut off at the beginning of the process), place it inside the top of the main part of the bottle, and tape it in place. This part acts as a funnel as rain comes in and drops down into the larger part of the gauge. After it rains, the amount of rainfall can be measured (in quarter-inches or even inches) by how far up the water level in the bottle has risen from the line marked with a zero (0).

Playing with Water

Read the book *Anna Carries Water* by Olive Senior, a quick, accessible story set in Jamaica. Young Anna struggles to learn to carry water on her head; she must be persistent. The brilliant colors and theme of perseverance in this story lend themselves to a musical water activity.

Fill identical glass jars with varying levels of water, and add food coloring to each jar to set them apart from one another. Use a metal spoon to tap the outside of each jar, listening to the different pitches. Invite participants to create songs or even attempt to play familiar tunes on the jars. (This may require adjusting the amount of water in the jars, in order to attain specific notes; a pitch pipe or another tuning tool can be helpful, and participants will need to use perseverance in order to succeed.)

Density Rainbow

Share the book *Water: How We Can Protect Our Freshwater* by Catherine Barr, a nonfiction introduction to the increasing scarcity of clean water, the water cycle, and water issues around the world.

Take inspiration from the book's water cycle content, as well as the distinction between freshwater and saltwater, by creating "density rainbows." Fill six identical empty, clear plastic bottles (such as disposable water bottles) with water. Add food coloring to dye each bottle's water a different color of the rainbow (from red to purple). Now, mix salt into five of the bottles: two teaspoons into the orange water, four teaspoons into the yellow, six into the green, eight into the blue, and ten into the purple. Seal one end of a clear drinking straw with your thumb, and insert the open end half an inch into the red water (which has no salt in it). Remove your thumb very briefly, then replace it before moving the straw to the orange bottle, inserting the open end a full inch below the surface. Briefly lift your thumb, then replace before moving to the yellow bottle, where you'll insert the open end one and a half inches under water. Continue in this manner through the rainbow. Because of the varying densities of the different colors of water, a rainbow is built in the straw!

TWEEN PROGRAMS

Water Relay Race

Around the world, water is transported in a variety of ways. Share the book *Water Day* by Margarita Engle, in which a young Cuban narrator and her friends and family anticipate and celebrate the water man's weekly visit, via horse-drawn cart, to their village. Give participants an opportunity to try moving water in creative ways with a water relay race. Start each team with a uniform bucket of water at one end of a room or field. At the other end, place one empty bucket per team. Challenge participants to transport their water from the full bucket to the empty one—without moving the buckets at all. Offer tools such as sponges, spoons, and turkey basters for carrying the water.

If you like, measure each team's water at the end of the activity to find out how much water was transported and how much was lost along the way. Which team was fastest? Which team lost the least water? Which of these is most important?

Walking Water

Water (and the pollutants or additives it holds) flows quickly. Share the book *We Are Water Protectors* by Carole Lindstrom, featuring an unnamed Anishinaabe girl who speaks out about the dangers of water pollution. The girl issues a call for action against the "black snake" (oil pipe) that damages land, water, plants, and animals.

See the movement of water—and its additives—for yourself in this experiment. Set five identical clear plastic cups in a line. Fill the first, third, and fifth cups halfway with water. Add a few drops of food coloring to each cup of water, yielding one cup in each of the primary colors. Fold four half-sheets of paper towel into long, thin rectangles. Arrange the towels so that one end is in a water cup and one end is in an empty cup, essentially linking the entire line of cups with paper towels. Watch as the water moves across the towels, carrying food coloring into the adjacent cups.

Clean That Up!

Host a discussion of the middle-grade novel *Flush* by Carl Hiaasen. In this book, Noah's dad lands in jail trying to prove that a casino boat is flushing raw sewage into the harbor. Noah, convinced that his dad is right, joins forces with a few quirky friends to continue the quest to expose the casino.

Provide a bucket of water containing additives of different sizes and textures, such as sticks, mud, ping-pong balls, and marbles, along with a variety of supplies, like spoons, sponges, cotton balls, fabric, coffee filters, bottles, and bowls. Challenge participants to design a water filtration device that will yield the cleanest possible water.

Make this program into a three-part book club by holding two additional meetings. Discuss *The Friendship Lie* by Rebecca Donnelly and *Hello from Renn Lake* by Michele Weber Hurwitz and then repeat the water challenge, each time with a new combination of tools and additives.

Water Magic

Hold a book club focused on *Stinky Cecil in Operation Pond Rescue* by Paige Braddock. Readers will meet American Toad Cecil, who finds out that a freeway project threatens the pond that he and several other animals call home. This graphic novel follows the adventures of Cecil and his friends as they take things into their own hands . . . or into their webbed feet, as the case may be.

While a group of rogue animals securing the future of a pond may seem impossible, keeping a paper towel dry underwater might also seem out of the question. Experience the seemingly impossible with this experiment. Crumple a dry paper towel and stuff it into the bottom of a glass or clear cup. Turn the glass upside down and slowly submerge it in a bowl or tub of colored water (use a few drops of food coloring to create this). Even when the glass is completely underwater, the towel inside remains dry!

TEEN PROGRAMS

Testing the Waters

Discuss the book *Not a Drop to Drink* by Mindy McGinnis. Sixteen-year-old Lynn lives in a dystopian world; diseases are plentiful, but clean water isn't, so Lynn must work to defend her family's pond. When their water source—and the people closest to them—are threatened, Lynn must do whatever it takes to survive.

What's in your water? Collect water samples from various sources into sterilized jars. Consider the library bathroom's tap, a rain spout after a downpour, a puddle, and a lake or pond. If you like, invite participants to bring water from home. Purchase water testing strips to measure the water samples' pH, hardness, and alkalinity. Challenge groups of participants to find out what these terms mean, then invite them to teach one another. Set up a microscope to examine water samples up close. If resources allow, provide take-home kits for participants to use to test the water in their homes.

Tie Dye

Hold a discussion of *A Long Walk to Water* by Linda Sue Park, told as tandem stories of two eleven-year-old Sudanese children. Salva, one of Sudan's "lost boys," whose village was attacked by rebel soldiers in 1985, and Nya, whose days are spent fetching water for her family from miles away, find their lives intertwined. Look for Park's companion picture book, *Nya's Long Walk.*

In the book, the lives of Salva and Nya mix together in unexpected ways. Tie-dye art involves colors combining and interacting, thanks to water, sometimes in surprising shapes and shades. Use a traditional dye approach to create one-of-a-kind shirts, totes, or other items.

Will It Float? Predictions Board

Feature the environmental thriller *Water Wars* by Cameron Stracher, set in a parched world, where water is precious enough to be fought over and millions are dying from dehydration, disease, and hunger. When Kai, the son of a wealthy water driller, disappears, his friends Vera and Will set out to find and rescue him—encountering pirates, ecoterrorists, and the corrupt heart of the water conspiracy.

In the book, Vera, Will, and Kai had to make choices and take risks. Enlist the help of teens at this book discussion to create a "Will It Float?" passive programming station, where library visitors are faced with choices (though for much lower stakes than the characters'). As a group, collect items that will be tested to determine their buoyancy. Take a photo of each item (an instant camera works well), and on a sheet of butcher paper or a bulletin board, create a simple table. Place the items to be tested on the left side of the table, each in its own row. Add two columns, labeled "Floats" and "Doesn't Float." Include brief instructions inviting library visitors to make tally marks in one column or the other, reflecting their predictions. After a few weeks (possibly at your next club or group meeting, if this is part of an ongoing program), test each item to see if it floats or not, videotaping the tests. Post the videos and results on social media.

Who's Thirsty?

Hold a book discussion based around *Thirst* by Varsha Bajaj, the story of twelve-year-old Minni, who lives in a part of Mumbai where water access is limited. When Minni learns that wealthy thieves are stealing water from her neighborhood, she faces a big—and dangerous—decision.

Ahead of time or with the help of the group during the program, create profiles of individuals or groups who need water. These might include a farmer who needs water for her crops, a child who needs water to bathe, or a doctor who needs water for hand-washing and instrument cleaning. Then tell participants that they are in charge of an imaginary water supply, and they can only choose a certain number of requests to grant. How will they decide which requests to grant? Which requests are the most important? What happens to the people who don't receive water?

PASSIVE PROGRAMS

Create a book display featuring water-related materials for all ages. Find books for the display in your fiction and nonfiction sections. Near the display, set up a passive programming station, where patrons are invited to engage in activities any time they're at the library. Try the following activities at your passive programming station.

Batik-Inspired Water Resist Art

Draw with crayons (be sure not to use washable crayons) on paper, then paint over the drawing with watercolors. For easy clean-up, try refillable daubers and liquid watercolors. Consider this project for a passive programming station that patrons can visit during any of the library's open hours.

Float It!

While this activity may seem elementary, any age will enjoy it. Provide a variety of materials, and challenge library visitors to build structures capable of floating in water. How many pennies will each structure support before sinking? Make this a passive program by setting up a "Build a Boat" station, where patrons can create their (hopefully) floatable structures before handing them in at the service desk. Later, take a video of a staff member testing each structure, and post the video on the library's website and social media pages.

Will It Float?

See the teen program "Will It Float? Predictions Board" earlier in this chapter for instructions.

COMMUNITY CONNECTIONS

- Identify local, national, or international organizations that support clean water and hygiene initiatives. Work with teens or tweens at your library to select one or two organizations to support through fund-raising and information sharing.
- Invite a local expert (try the water or sewer utility) to talk with patrons about water usage, local water issues, and inside info on water and sanitation. Ask about the possibility of an in-person or virtual field trip to a local water facility.

- Partner with a local hardware store to host a build-your-own rain barrel program for all ages. Before and during the program, discuss the benefits of rain barrels and the best ways to use one.
- Encourage teens and tweens to spread the word about water issues by creating posters, videos, and other public education tools that share facts and strategies related to clean water. Invite them to create a book display or bulletin board at the library, or give them the opportunity to include an article in the library's newsletter.

NOTES

1. United Nations, Department of Economic and Social Affairs, Sustainable Development, "Goals, 6," https://sdgs.un.org/goals/goal6.
2. United Nations, *The Sustainable Development Goals Report 2020* (United Nations, 2020), https://unstats.un.org/sdgs/report/2020/.

7 Affordable and Clean Energy

Sustainable development goal 7: Ensure access to affordable, reliable, sustainable and modern energy for all.[1]

EVERY DAY, WE rely on energy to meet our basic needs. Growing and cooking safe and healthy food, running businesses, maintaining health care facilities, and accessing education all hinge on the availability of energy. Unfortunately, many people still live without access to electricity, and even more rely on unsustainable energy sources that pollute the environment and affect the entire world. The seventh sustainable development goal focuses on renewable energy sources and making sure these are accessible for everyone.[2] Books and activities related to sustainable energy and the ways we use energy in our everyday lives will spark thought and conversation around this goal.

FAMILY PROGRAMS

Sun Art Prints

Harness the power of the sun by making one-of-a-kind solar art prints. You'll need sun art paper (available online or at craft stores), clear acrylic sheets the same size as the paper (or larger), and a variety of objects, such as keys, leaves, string, or coins. On a sheet of paper, arrange the items, leaving some space between them. Lay the acrylic sheet over the arrangement, and bring everything out into the sunlight. Within three to five minutes, you'll notice the paper turning blue, except where the objects are blocking the light; these areas of the paper remain white. Remove the acrylic sheet and all the objects, and place the paper in a tub or pan of water, submerging it completely. (Water halts the chemical process and fixes the images on the paper permanently.) After one minute, remove the paper from the water and hang it up to dry. While the projects dry, share books such as *Sun! One in a Billion* by Stacy McAnulty or *Saving the Sun* by Emma Pearl.

Light the Way: Solar-Powered Jar Lanterns

Combine this project with the "Sun Art Prints" project, or host a separate solar-powered lantern workshop. Books such as *Windows* by Julia Denos and *The House in the Night* by Susan Marie Swanson work well with this project. Provide clear jars, such as Mason jars, paint brushes, and glow-in-the-dark paint. Invite families to decorate the insides of the jars with the paint. If you like, also provide materials, such as wire and beads, for making lantern handles. When the jars are exposed to the sun, the paint will store some of the sun's power; when the jars are viewed in the dark, you'll see this solar power in the form of a glow from the paint.

Windy Days

Provide two hands-on activities for families to explore wind power: simple pinwheels and wind vanes. Create wind vanes using everyday materials, following the instructions online from PBS Kids.[3] For pinwheels, paper, scissors, coloring supplies, pencils, and pushpins are all you'll need. Cut a 6-inch square from paper or cardstock, and decorate it as you choose. Fold it diagonally, right bottom corner to top left corner, then unfold, and fold diagonally again, left bottom corner to top right. Unfold, and notice the two creases you've created. Cut along each crease, starting at the corner, creating three-inch slits toward the center. Arrange the square so that one slit is facing you. Punch a hole just to the right of that slit. Now turn the paper 90 degrees and repeat. Continue until you've punched four holes, one next to each slit. Fold the punched corners toward one another, overlapping so that the holes line up. Insert a pushpin through all four holes at once and then into the eraser end of a pencil. Hold the pencil in your hand and watch the wind spin the paper! Before, during, or after these activities, share books such as *Jeremy Worried About the Wind* by Pamela Butchart, *Kate, Who Tamed The Wind* by Liz Garton Scanlon, *Energy Island* by Allan Drummond, or *I Am the Wind* by Michael Karg.

Go with the Flow: Make a Water Wheel

Create and test a water wheel. Many ideas and patterns for these exist online; try the video tutorial by the Children's Museum of Houston.[4] Accompany this project with books such as *Hey, Water!* by Antoinette Portis or *Hydropower* by Mary Boone.

TWEEN PROGRAMS

Got Energy? Book Club

Hold a multipart book club, or choose one book and activity for a one-time event. At an introductory meeting, or as a supplement during each meeting, share *Planet Power: Explore the World's Renewable Energy* by Stacy Clark or other books from your collection about sustainable energy.

Wind Power

Discuss the young readers' edition of *The Boy Who Harnessed the Wind* by William Kamkwamba and Bryan Mealer, a memoir of a boy growing up in Malawi who, during a drought that threatened his village's farms, created a windmill out of scrap metal to power the delivery of water.

Together, harness the wind in your area by building kites. Provide materials such as old newspapers and clean plastic bags. Show a few short online kite-building tutorials, and challenge participants to create a kite of their own design. If space and weather permit, try the kites out!

Solar Power

Share and discuss *Iqbal and His Ingenious Idea: How a Science Project Helps One Family and the Planet* by Elizabeth Suneby. In Bangladesh during the monsoon season, Iqbal's mother cooks over an open fire, indoors. The fire's smoke pollutes the air, making breathing difficult. Iqbal sets out to design a stove that works without producing smoke as part of a sustainability-themed science fair.

If you like, introduce a book or two involving hot dogs from your collection. Tweens will wonder what hot dogs have to do with solar power . . . until you tell them that they'll be building solar hot dog ovens. Many websites offer instructions for this; try the Cub Scout Ideas design.[5] Be sure to ask about food allergies, and purchase hot dogs or a vegetarian option that are already fully cooked.

Water Power

Discuss a water- or dam-themed book, such as *The Wild River and the Great Dam: The Construction of Hoover Dam and the Vanishing Colorado River* by Simon

Boughton. Then get busy with hands-on water power experimentation. Try the "Water Power" activity by The Science Kiddo; you'll want to try this one outdoors if possible.[6] Also consider preparing the materials ahead of time for maximum hands-on time.

Pedal Power

Share the book *Crunch* by Leslie Connor, about Dewey, whose parents run a bike shop. While Mom and Dad are out of town, a gasoline shortage means that Dewey and his siblings are not only on their own—they're also the focal point of the community, as everyone suddenly needs a bicycle.

Invite a local bike shop to send a mechanic or other representative to your program to talk with tweens about biking and the energy benefits of traveling by bike. If possible, have the guest talk about basic bike maintenance, and guide participants through putting together small bike kits so that each person can take a kit home. These could be small cloth bags that can be carried in a backpack or strapped under a bike seat, and they might include supplies for changing a tire, a QR code to a tire-changing video, sanitizing wipes, a mini flashlight, Band-Aids, and other items.

TEEN PROGRAMS

Wild Winds

Highlight books from your collection about renewable energy that focus on wind power, or discuss a title that involves wind-powered travel, such as *The Mermaid, the Witch, and the Sea* by Maggie Tokuda-Hall, in which the characters travel by sea, using the wind to blow the sails.

Invite participants to build an anemometer (an instrument used to measure wind speed). NASA provides instructions online; try these, or use them as a jumping-off point for creating original designs.[7] After the instruments have been built, put them to the test by fanning the air with large pieces of cardstock or bellows. Experiment with various sizes, shapes, and arrangements of pieces to see which design moves the most quickly and which moves the most slowly (or not at all).

An alternate or additional activity is a build-your-own wind turbine. Science Buddies has posted instructions for creating a turbine that actually performs work (lifting items).[8] Try powering it with a fan or bellows and experiment with different variables, such as the size and shape of the blades.

Get Cooking!

Highlight your cookbook collection or discuss a book with culinary-related content such as *With the Fire on High* by Elizabeth Acevedo. Build solar-powered ovens that teens can try out and take home. Many ideas and designs are available online; try the Pizza Box Solar Oven plans from Science Buddies.[9] If you like, provide a variety of ingredients and invite teens to make their own solar-cooked delicacies. Be sure that anything you offer is safe to eat without being cooked, and inquire about food allergies during program registration.

Light Up the Library

Create solar-powered lamps for teens to take home or display in the library. Combine 3D printing and circuitry with a project from Makezine.com or choose something lower-tech, such as an idea featured on the Creative Cain Cabin blog.[10] If a sunny day presents itself during your program, try charging up the lamps outside and then trying them out in a darkened area of the library.

What Do You Know? Renewable Energy Game

Set up a game show-style activity with questions and challenges based around renewable energy. Alternatively, invite participants to work in small groups to design original board games with renewable energy themes. Try these ideas, or come up with your own:

- Energy Charades: Prepare notecards with words related to renewable energy on them. Challenge teams of participants to act out the words, leading others to guess the words on the notecards.
- Data Crunch: Ask number-oriented questions, such as "How many gallons of crude oil are needed to create one gallon of gasoline?" (two) or "In what year was the first wind turbine built?" (1887) and have participants write their answers down and reveal them before the answer is given.

PASSIVE PROGRAMS

Blowing in the Wind

Invite patrons to experiment with wind power. Set up a station with hand-powered fans and bellows, along with scarves, ribbons, paper, and other light objects. Encourage visitors to try creating wind to make the objects move.

Take-Home Updraft Towers

Provide an opportunity for library visitors to build simple updraft towers, which demonstrate the potential for solar power to move objects. Many ideas and tutorials for this are available online; try the Science Buddies design or another that fits your space, patrons, and resources.[11] Better yet, try more than one, and invite patrons to compare their experiences with each style.

Solar Power Repurposing Challenge

Ideas abound online for reusing and repurposing solar-powered yard stake lights and solar puck lights, which can be purchased online or at dollar stores. While these lights do present sustainability concerns themselves, they are an accessible tool for learning about solar power. Distribute solar-powered yard stake lights or puck lights and ideas for repurposing them, such as lit terrariums, solar chandeliers, or solar-powered costume elements (such as light-up sabers). Invite community members to create something new and original with their lights and either return them to the library for display or submit photos for an online gallery of solar power creations.

Test Your Energy Knowledge

Create a bulletin board or reproducible worksheet-style true or false quiz for patrons to complete, featuring statements about energy. Try these examples to get you started:

- Coal is a type of fossil fuel (true)
- Fossil fuels are easily replaced (false)
- Solar power can only be gathered on sunny days (false)

COMMUNITY CONNECTIONS

- Invite local experts on renewable energy to share information at the library. Host one-time programs featuring one or two guest speakers per event, or plan a larger renewable energy fair, where experts host tables or booths to answer questions and talk with patrons.

- Contact organizations in your area, such as community bicycle share programs, and inquire about partnering with the organization. The library might offer passes for bikes that can be checked out, or the organization may be willing to offer coupons or gift certificates that can be used as prizes or giveaways at programs.
- Hold bike tune-ups at the library, hosted by a local bike shop.

NOTES

1. United Nations, "Ensure Access to Affordable, Reliable, Sustainable and Modern Energy," www.un.org/sustainabledevelopment/energy/.
2. United Nations, "SDG 7 – Affordable and Clean Energy Reading List," www.un.org/sustainabledevelopment/sdgbookclub-7archive/.
3. PBS Kids, "Where Is the Wind Going? Try a DIY Weather Vane," October 11, 2019, www.pbs.org/parents/crafts-and-experiments/where-is-the-wind-going-try-a-diy-weather-vane.
4. Children's Museum Houston (@childrensmuseumhouston), "Build a Water Wheel," YouTube video, April 21, 2021, www.youtube.com/watch?v=tcD29ywvrs8.
5. Sherry Smothermon-Short, "How to Make an Easy Solar Hot Dog Cooker," Cub Scout Ideas, https://cubscoutideas.com/2699/solar-hot-dog-cooker/.
6. Crystal, "Water Power," The Science Kiddo, August 7, 2014, https://sciencekiddo.com/water-power/.
7. NASA, Aeronautics Research Mission Directorate, "Build an Anemometer," April 2020, www.nasa.gov/wp-content/uploads/2020/04/build_an_anemometer.pdf.
8. Science Buddies, "Make the Wind Work for You!" May 3, 2024, www.sciencebuddies.org/science-fair-projects/project-ideas/Aero_p040/aerodynamics-hydrodynamics/wind-turbine-design.
9. Teisha Rowland, "Build a Pizza Box Solar Oven," Science Buddies, www.sciencebuddies.org/stem-activities/solar-oven.
10. Debasish Dutta, "DIY Solar Bottle Lamp," *Make: Magazine*, February 16, 2023, https://makezine.com/projects/diy-solar-bottle-lamp/; Dawn, "DIY Solar Lamp," Creative Cain Cabin, https://creativecaincabin.com/diy-solar-lamp/.
11. Svenja Lohner, "Build a Solar Updraft Tower," Science Buddies, www.sciencebuddies.org/stem-activities/solar-updraft-tower.

8

Decent Work and Economic Growth

Sustainable development goal 8: Promote sustained, inclusive and sustainable economic growth, full and productive employment and decent work for all.[1]

THIS SUSTAINABLE DEVELOPMENT goal is focused on work and economic growth. All people deserve safe jobs that pay them enough to live healthy lives. Unsafe workplaces, lack of fair pay, and unfair hiring practices are realities in our world. By addressing these issues and working to change them, we can not only ensure that individuals have good, safe jobs, but also that workers and their families can access other sustainable development goals. For example, workplaces that grant time off for sickness allow workers to seek health care when needed, which is related to SDG 3. Adults who are paid fairly can afford to send their children to school equipped to learn (SDG 4). Explore SDG 8 with books and activities centered on equitable workplaces and meaningful work.

FAMILY PROGRAMS

Basket of Bangles

Share the book *A Basket of Bangles: How a Business Begins* by Ginger Howard, about a woman in Bangladesh who joined forces with a few friends and started a business, thereby changing their lives. Don't be fooled by the simple look of this book; deep conversation fodder waits between the covers. After the read-aloud, provide a variety of jewelry-making supplies, and invite participants to create bangles or other items of their choosing.

One Hen

Based on a true story, *One Hen: How One Small Loan Made a Big Difference* by Katie Smith Milway introduces readers to Kojo, a Ghanaian boy who must drop out of school to help his mother collect and sell firewood after the death of his father. His mother becomes the recipient of a community loan, and she gives a small amount to Kojo. He uses the money to buy a hen, and within a year, he has a flock of twenty-five chickens. Kojo earns enough to return to school and changes his family's life completely.

After sharing this book, offer chicken-related activities, such as folding an origami hen or making a clucking sound instrument. To do this, poke a small hole in the bottom of a plastic cup. Thread a cotton string through the hole, and, turning the cup upright as if you're going to drink out of it, tie a paper clip to the end of the string that extends out under the cup. Set the cup aside and dampen a paper towel, then fold it several times until it reaches a size of approximately three inches by one inch. Pick up the cup, holding it upside down (so the paper clip is facing the ceiling) in one hand. In the other hand, hold the paper towel rectangle so that one end is on your thumb and the other is on your forefinger. Grasp the string near the cup's mouth, pinching thumb and forefinger together as if to make a sandwich: finger, towel, string, towel, thumb. Squeeze the string as you pull downward in short bursts. You'll hear a clucking noise as the cup amplifies the vibrations of the string. If you like, add construction paper beaks and googly eyes to complete the chicken look.

Make Some Cents

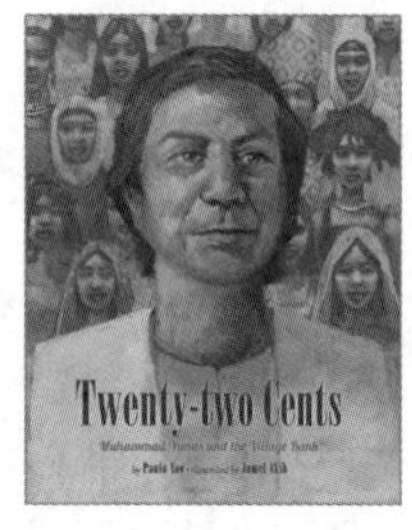

Read the book *Twenty-Two Cents: Muhammad Yunus and the Village Bank* by Paula Yoo, a biography of the Nobel Prize winner who developed the practice of micro-lending. Muhammad grew up in Bangladesh and became an economics professor. He met a woman who needed to borrow a very small amount of money to fund her business, and no bank would lend it to her, an uneducated woman. Her only option was to pursue a corrupt lender. Muhammad established a bank that provided loans to individuals like the woman he had met, so that they could afford to build their businesses.

Take inspiration from the small amounts of money referenced in the book and teach participants the Disappearing Coin magic trick. Invite families to create the supplies for this trick and practice it before going home. For each magician, you'll need:

- One sheet of construction paper, any color
- One clear plastic cup
- A glue stick
- Scissors
- A pencil
- A scarf or handkerchief
- A coin (consider using coins from around the world)

Place the cup upside down on one corner of the construction paper, and trace around the cup's opening. Cut the circle out, and trim the remaining part of the paper into a rectangle (so the cut-out circle isn't obvious). Glue the paper circle onto the cup's rim. Place the cup, rim-side down, onto the paper rectangle. Viewers won't be able to tell that the cup has paper glued to the rim; all they'll see is a clear cup sitting upside down. Tell the audience that you're going to make a coin disappear. Place a coin on the paper rectangle, next to the cup. Place the handkerchief or scarf over the cup, say some magic-sounding words, and move the cup over the coin, concealing the money beneath the paper secretly glued to the cup's rim. Remove the scarf or handkerchief, revealing the coin's absence. Then reverse the trick, making the coin reappear with a few more magic words and a flourish of the scarf.

Building Together

Someone Builds the Dream by Lisa Wheeler is an exploration and celebration of workers whose labors have collaborative results—bridges, books, wind farms, amusement parks, and more. Provide your choice of building materials, such as blocks, cardboard boxes, PVC pipes and connectors, or other items. Invite participants to build together to create anything they choose. At the close of the program, ask each family to tell about what they built and reflect on their building process.

TWEEN PROGRAMS

Read and Watch

Encourage participants to read the comic version of *Kiki's Delivery Service* by Hayao Miyazaki, about a young witch who starts a courier service. Host a discussion of the book, and talk especially about the work Kiki was doing. Ask participants how they would expect to be compensated if they did a job like Kiki's. How would they set their prices? What would they consider when deciding how much to charge? Follow the book discussion with a showing of the Studio Ghibli movie of the same title.

Checking In

Front Desk by Kelly Yang is the first in a book series featuring Mia Tang, whose entire family (including Mia and her immigrant parents) lives and works in a motel. Mia dreams of being a writer one day, but for now, she has bigger things to worry about—like the motel's owner finding out her family's secret.

Some hotels and motels fold towels and washcloths into intricate shapes, such as animals and flowers. Provide towels of varying sizes and give tweens a chance to try some fancy folding. If you like, print QR codes ahead of time that connect to online instructions.

Play on the theme of keys by setting up a system of padlocks and keys. Make sure that each lock has a key (and if you like, add a few extra keys to add to the challenge). On each lock (or on a tag attached to the lock), write a riddle or question. On the corresponding key (or a tag attached to the key), write the answer. Place prizes, such as bookmarks, stickers, or other treats, inside a small box. Lock the box—or a cable wrapped around the box—with one of the locks. Place this box inside a slightly larger box, and lock this box with another lock. Continue adding larger, locked boxes. Lay out all of the keys on a table, and invite tweens to unlock the boxes by identifying the correct answers—and thereby, the correct keys—and opening the locks.

Smooth Operator

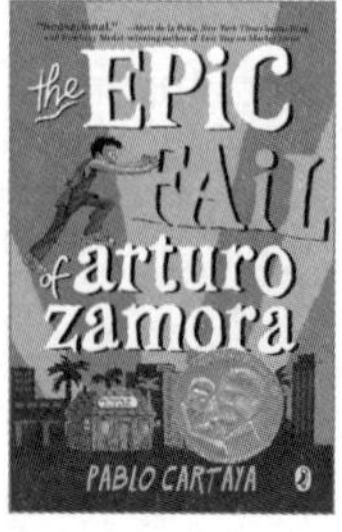

The Epic Fail of Arturo Zamora by Pablo Cartaya is about a thirteen-year-old who loves mango smoothies, helps out in his family's restaurant, and has a new love interest. When a land developer arrives, Arturo knows he must take action to save the restaurant—and the town. Follow a discussion of this book with a smoothie-making activity (alternatively, ask a local smoothie shop to donate drinks), a nod to Arturo's favorite beverage.

Odd Jobs

Share books from your collection about unusual careers (try *World's Coolest Jobs* by Anna Brett), and explore them with participants. Then ask tweens to work in pairs or small groups to select a job from one of the books and write a want ad, as though they were the employer advertising for potential employees. In the ad, ask them not to name the job specifically, but to provide enough clues so that other participants could guess what the job might be. Have groups read their ads aloud, and encourage others to identify the job. Collect the ads to use as part of a passive program (see the passive program "Odd Jobs Ad Board" in this chapter).

TEEN PROGRAMS

What's Your Vision?

Teens are at a perfect age to begin thinking about the jobs they may wish to pursue. Provide withdrawn magazines, scissors, glue, cardstock or poster board, and invite participants to create their own career vision board. They might include specifics, such as an exact job title, or they might choose to name general fields or areas of interest. Geographical area, scheduling considerations, and compensation may also be factors reflected on the vision boards. If possible, invite a career counselor, a representative from a local community college, or a high school counselor to the program to talk with teens about their vision boards and practical steps they could take to make their career dreams come true.

Get a Job!

Host a job fair where teens and potential employers can connect. Format this as an open house, where employers are available to provide information and talk with visitors, or choose a speed networking model. Small, round tables work well for speed networking; use these if they're available. Seat one employer at each table, and add two or three additional chairs. Have teens begin at the table of their choice, where they'll ask questions and receive information. After four minutes, sound a chime, and have participants move to the next table while employers remain to greet the next group.

Practice Makes Perfect

Hold a preparatory program for teens, including a resume review workshop and mock interviews. Ask local employers, career counselors, or others to help as experts who can provide tips on resumes and give feedback on interviews. If you like, offer a Resume 101 program for teens who wish to begin writing their resumes from scratch.

Work It! Book Club

Host a book club with a theme of jobs and careers. Try these titles, or look for others in your collection:

- *Chloe and the Kaishao Boys* by Mae Coyiuto, featuring an aspiring animator whose family has other plans
- *The Cost of Knowing* by Brittney Morris, an evocative, mature book with themes of business ownership and economics
- *The Education of Margot Sanchez* by Lillian Rivera, about Margot, whose choices (uninvited borrowing of her dad's credit card) lead to what feels like indentured servitude in her family's grocery store, ushering in a series of tough decisions related to social status, Margot's future, and the morals she lives by
- *Everything Leads to You* by Nina LaCour, centered around Emi, a production design intern in Los Angeles, whose discovery of a mysterious letter prompts an adventure
- *Geekerella* by Ashley Poston, introducing Elle, who uses her wages from her food truck job to attempt to make her dreams of meeting a famous actor come true
- *The Peach Rebellion* by Wendelin Van Draanen, a historical novel about the complicated friendship between three girls: a peach picker, a peach farm owner's daughter, and a wealthy banker's daughter
- *With the Fire on High* by Elizabeth Acevedo, about an aspiring and talented chef who faces difficult decisions

PASSIVE PROGRAMS

Odd Jobs Ad Board

On a wall or bulletin board, post the advertisements written by tweens in the "Odd Jobs" program (in the "Tween Programs" section). Invite library visitors to guess the job that each ad is seeking to fill. If you like, set up lift-the-flap answer reveals, or have patrons write their responses on sticky notes and add them to the wall next to the corresponding advertisements.

What's My Job?

Challenge patrons to connect book characters with their job titles. Try these industrious characters to get you started:

- Atticus Finch (attorney)
- Guy Montag (firefighter)
- Sam Spade (private investigator)
- Mikael Blomkvist (journalist)
- Willy Wonka (candy maker)
- Mary Poppins (nanny)

Dream Big

Hang a large sheet of butcher paper on a wall, and place colorful markers or pens nearby. Post a prompt such as "What's Your Dream Job?" and encourage library visitors to add their ideal careers to the paper.

Career Quiz

Post a trivia quiz (and other questions) about jobs, employment, or careers, and invite library visitors to submit their answers. Questions might include:

- Are archaeologists most likely to study the past, the present, or the future?
- Buzz Aldrin, John Glenn, and Ellen Ochoa all had the same career. What was it?
- Where might a cosmetologist work?

COMMUNITY CONNECTIONS

- Invite guests from the community to talk about their jobs. Include business owners, supervisors, human resource specialists, front-line workers, and behind-the-scenes personnel. Look for self-employed individuals, as well as staff members from large businesses. Host a series of programs, each featuring one type of worker, or hold a larger program with a panel representing a diverse range of employment experiences.
- Create a physical or online job board, where library visitors can connect with employment opportunities in the community. This may be a great opportunity to partner with the local Chamber of Commerce.

NOTE

1. United Nations, Department of Economic and Social Affairs, Sustainable Development, "Goals, 8," https://sdgs.un.org/goals/goal8.

9

Industry, Innovation, and Infrastructure

Sustainable development goal 9: Build resilient infrastructure, promote inclusive and sustainable industrialization and foster innovation.[1]

THE NINTH SUSTAINABLE development goal addresses safe and efficient transportation, connectivity to water, electricity, and the internet, innovative structures and systems, and advances in technology and engineering. Naturally, this goal overlaps with many other SDGs. Books and activities centered around building, inventing, transportation, and other forms of relatable infrastructure, industry, and innovation will bring this goal to life for library patrons.

FAMILY PROGRAMS

From Here to There

Share books related to innovations in transportation, such as *Means of Transport That Almost Changed the World* by Tom Velcovsky and Stepanka Sekaninova, and *If I Built a Car* by Chris Van Dusen. Provide a variety of art supplies, and invite participants to work together to build vehicles of their choosing. Add a ramp made from a large piece of cardboard propped up on one side, and have families test their creations. If time allows, ask each family to explain the features of their invention to the group.

Lift It!

Share books about up-and-down motion, such as *Lift* by Minh Lê or *Fox & Chick: Up and Down and Other Stories* by Sergio Ruzzier. Together, experiment with pulleys and levers; Inspiration Laboratories and Science Buddies both offer accessible projects for this.[2] If you're ready to get fancy, try building a hydraulic lift using the instructions by Teach Beside Me.[3]

Questioneers Party

Celebrate Andrea Beaty's *Questioneers* series, which includes picture books, chapter books, and nonfiction books (*The Why Files*). Looking for décor inspiration? A red background with large white polka dots evokes Ada Twist's signature outfit. At the party, provide a variety of STEAM activities (try the activities in this chapter, or find ideas in your library's collection or online). Draw inspiration from the DuPage Children's Museum's hands-on "Questioneers" exhibit.[4]

Secret Alarm

Wouldn't it be fun to make a tiny alarm? One so small that no one would suspect it was there? Great news: this is possible! Use the instructions provided by PBS Kids to guide families in building teeny tiny alarms.[5] The only difficult part will be deciding where to hide them!

TWEEN PROGRAMS

Find Your Way

Tell the Greek myth of the labyrinth, highlighting your mythology collection. Talk about the labyrinth and how it may have been designed. Give tweens an opportunity to build their very own cardboard marble mazes using the ideas provided online by the Center for Architecture.[6]

Build a Bridge

Discuss a book involving bridges, such as *The Bridge Home* by Padma Venkatraman, *The Bridge Battle* by Jacqueline Davies, or, for nonfiction fans, *This Bridge Will Not Be Gray* by Dave Eggers. Working in pairs or small groups, give tweens paper and clear tape. Challenge them to use only these supplies to build a bridge between two books. Find instructions and inspiration online from Science Buddies.[7]

Stack and Stand

Use cups for two hands-on engineering activities. During this program, feature books about building and construction.

- Try a variety of cup-stacking challenges. You'll need cups that are uniform in size and shape, as well as a flat, sturdy surface, such as a table. The Speedstacks website offers many ideas for stacking challenges.[8] Make these collaborative by having tweens work as a team, or hold a tournament to determine the fastest stacker in the group.
- Ask participants if they think they could stand on a paper cup. Give them an opportunity to try; they'll probably end up flattening the cup. Using the instructions from Science Sparks, guide participants in finding a way to successfully stand on paper cups.[9]

Squish It!

Experiment with circuitry using conductive modeling dough and a few supplies. Kits or separate components can be purchased from Squishy Circuits, or you can make your own dough and use components found elsewhere; the website Makerspaces.com provides step-by-step instructions.[10]

TEEN PROGRAMS

Map Art

Provide old maps, such as those found in withdrawn atlases or almanacs, and use them to create art projects. A self-healing cutting mat and a rotary cutter may be helpful, as well as a paper cutter. Scissors, glue, string, hole punches, and other art supplies add to the possibilities. Pull origami books from your collection, and encourage teens to cut maps into perfect squares and fold their choice of items. One-of-a-kind buttons, coasters, greeting cards, magnets, and bunting are delightful map projects for teens to make; they'll probably have many of their own ideas, too.

Cardboard in Motion

Use basic supplies and simple mechanics to build cardboard automata, an artistic way to explore machine elements, including levers, gears, and cams. The Exploratorium provides detailed instructions and ideas online.[11] If you like, pair this activity with a discussion of the all-ages favorite *The Invention of Hugo Cabret* by Brian Selznick or a screening of the movie version, called *Hugo*.

Lights On!

Soft circuits present the opportunity for teens to make light-up bracelets, plushies, and other cloth items. UC Santa Cruz has created a step-by-step guide for soft circuitry; use these instructions to get you started, and be prepared for teens to come up with new ideas once they understand the basics.[12] Soft circuits may work well as a multipart program or ongoing club, as many options exist for this project, and creations can be time-intensive.

After Hours Domino Marathon

If possible, hold this program after the library is closed (alternatively, hold it in a closed-off area, such as a programming room). Provide dominoes, withdrawn hardcover books (which can serve as large dominoes), golf balls, bells and strings, and other materials that could be used to build a giant domino course. Together, plan the course and any special features, such as:

- A book sets a golf ball rolling down a length of PVC pipe; at the end of the pipe, a domino waits to be knocked down by the ball.
- A small bell hangs over the course, between two dominoes or books. When the items fall, the bell rings.

PASSIVE PROGRAMS

On the Go

Set out a bin of PVC pipes, connectors, cardboard, and matchbox cars, along with a display of books about cars and roads. Encourage library visitors to experiment with sending the cars through the pipes, creating bridges, and getting cars from one space to another. You may be surprised at the many ages that enjoy this activity.

Find Your Way

Create a simple map of the library, marking several spots on the map with stars or other symbols. At each of the physical locations that corresponds with a star, place a rubber stamp or a specially shaped hole punch. Encourage participants to make their way around the library, using the map as a guide, and collect stamps or punches from each station. If you like, provide a small prize to patrons who complete the challenge.

Any Time Is Building Time

Set out a basket of simple blocks, along with an invitation to build. Depending on your space and needs, consider hollow cardboard blocks or foam blocks. Change out the building supplies every week or two, trading the blocks for less conventional building materials, such as tongue depressors, wooden spools, or other easy-to-access items.

Special Delivery

Postal services are one very visible form of infrastructure at work. Provide paper, envelopes, and a few art supplies, such as rubber stamps or stickers, and invite library visitors to create original cards or stationery and write notes or letters to friends, family members, or others. If you like, include an option for mail to be delivered by the library to schools (be sure that children or caregivers clearly write the name of the teacher and the school on the envelope for easy delivery).

COMMUNITY CONNECTIONS

- Invite guest speakers such as builders, engineers, postal workers, construction workers, contractors, electricians, truck drivers, and plumbers who can provide insight into the inner workings of some of the infrastructure we use daily.
- Provide community maps, highlighting places of interest such as museums, playgrounds, schools, and bike paths.

NOTES

1. United Nations, Department of Economic and Social Affairs, Sustainable Development, "Goals, 9," https://sdgs.un.org/goals/goal9.
2. Inspiration Laboratories, "Simple Machines for Kids: Levers and Pulleys," July 15, 2013, https://inspirationlaboratories.com/simple-machines-for-kids-levers-and-pulleys/; Science Buddies, "Teach about Simple Machines," September 12, 2022, www.sciencebuddies.org/blog/teach-simple-machines-experiments.
3. Teach Beside Me, "STEM Project – Build a Hydraulic Elevator," https://teachbesideme.com/stem-project-build-a-hydraulic-elevator/.
4. DuPage Children's Museum, "The Questioneers: Read. Question. Think. PLAY!" https://dupagechildrens.org/exhibit/questioneers/.

5. PBS Kids Design Squad Global, Build, "Hidden Alarm," https://pbskids.org/designsquad/build/hidden-alarm/.
6. Center for Architecture, "Design a Marble Maze Using Scrap Cardboard," www.centerforarchitecture.org/k-12/resources/design-a-marble-maze-using-scrap-cardboard/.
7. Science Buddies, "Build the Best Paper Bridge," www.sciencebuddies.org/stem-activities/build-best-bridge.
8. YouTube, Speed Stacks Inc, "Episode 1 – Introduction – Learn To Stack," December 17, 2014, www.speedstacks.com/learn/.
9. Science Sparks, "How Can You Stand on a Paper Cup without Breaking It?" April 29, 2020, www.science-sparks.com/how-can-you-stand-on-a-paper-cup-without-breaking-it/.
10. Squishy Circuits. https://squishycircuits.com; Makerspaces.com, "Squishy Circuits," www.makerspaces.com/squishy-circuits/.
11. Exploratorium, The Tinkering Studio, "Cardboard Automata," www.exploratorium.edu/sites/default/files/tinkering/files/Instructions/cardboard_automata_guide_final_screen.pdf.
12. UC Santa Cruz, Baskin Engineering, "Soft Circuits," https://users.soe.ucsc.edu/~emme/guide.pdf.

10

Reduced Inequalities

Sustainable development goal 10: Reduce inequality within and among countries.[1]

INEQUALITY TAKES MANY forms, as people around the world are commonly treated differently based on their gender, religion, race, age, country of origin, and other elements of their identities. Reducing inequality is a common theme among all of the SDGs, and the tenth goal gives us the chance to zero in on what equality and inequality look like in action. Books and activities that explore similarities, differences, and the experiences of migrants and refugees will bring this sustainable development goal to life.

FAMILY PROGRAMS

Breaking Down Walls

Offer the following as a series of programs, or as a longer, more involved one-time event.

Little Mouse

Share *Little Mouse and the Red Wall* by Britta Teckentrup, the story of a community of animals too fearful to explore what may lay beyond the wall, until one life-changing day when Mouse makes a bold move. Accompany this book with a simple related STEAM activity. Provide white paper cups, magnet wands, craft magnets (be sure they're attracted to the wands), and basic art supplies, including paper, scissors, markers, and glue or tape. Guide participants through these steps:

- Create a paper mouse that is small enough to easily fit inside the cup and that includes a craft magnet on the back or bottom.
- Decorate the cup (inside and out, if you choose) to look like a brick wall.

- Place your mouse inside the cup. Using a magnet wand held on the outside of the cup, attempt to help the mouse climb up and over the wall (the side of the cup will be sandwiched between the two magnets).

What Lies Beyond?

The Wall in the Middle of the Book by Jon Agee gives readers a glimpse of what's on each side of the wall—and insight into the unrealistic nature of the main character's fears and (incorrect) assumptions. Follow this book with a guessing game. On the floor or a table, set up cardboard partitions (these can be purchased from school supply stores or made with cardboard boxes; the creation of the partitions could even be part of the program). Seat one or more participants on both sides of each partition. Hand out small objects to individuals or groups on one side of each wall, and encourage patrons without objects to ask "yes or no" questions in an effort to determine the identity of the items.

Better Together

Share the book *Walls* by Brad Holdgrafer, an exploration of various types of walls and a celebration of breaking them down. Hold a hands-on challenge, illustrating the advantages of joined forces. Provide challenges, such as stacking cups, stringing beads on a pipe cleaner, or moving a stack of books from one table to another. Have participants attempt to complete the tasks by themselves, and then try again with the help of others. Discuss the difference in the two experiences.

Eggs-traordinary!

After the Fall (How Humpty Dumpty Got Up Again) by Dan Santat is an exploration of the famous egg's adventures after the incident of his fall. An egg drop challenge, such as the one described by the Griffin Museum of Science and Industry, makes the perfect accompaniment to this book.[2] You'll likely want to use cooked eggs in your program.

TWEEN PROGRAMS

Book Club for Equality

Host an ongoing book club focused on equality, interdependence, and related themes. Follow the book discussion with a large or small group activity that demonstrates the power of working together and the importance of access for everyone. Choose from the following lists of books and activities to create a dynamic book club that's sure to stir up conversation.

Books:

- *Amal Unbound* and its companion book *Omar Rising* by Aisha Saeed
- *The Boy at the Back of the Class* by Onjali Q. Raúf
- *Posted* by John David Anderson
- *Red, White, and Whole* by Rajani LaRocca

Activities:

- Use a few basic materials (plastic cups, rubber bands, and string) to create a teamwork challenge in which everyone must participate in order to meet the goal. Science4Us has posted illustrated step-by-step instructions; try this activity as an icebreaker, and look for ways it relates to the book at hand.[3]
- Set chairs numbering one less than the number of participants in a circle. The unseated player stands in the middle of the circle and says, "The wind blows for anyone who . . ." ending with a criterion that is true for them personally, such as "has a dog," "is an only child," and "loves pizza." All players who fit the criterion stand up and move to different chairs, while the player in the middle also sits down in a chair. The player left standing will be the next in the circle's center. Encourage participants to select criteria that are related to hobbies, interests, likes and dislikes, and family, rather than appearance. If you like, come up with a list of suggested criteria ahead of time that players can use for inspiration. This activity is perfect for recognizing similarities and differences, and for noticing that we each have a unique identity.
- Have participants stand in a circle with their hands out, palms facing the ceiling. Set a hula hoop so that it is resting on all players' fingertips, suspended horizontally in the air. Challenge the group to set the hoop on the ground without dropping or grasping the hoop—it must remain solely supported by their fingertips. Once tweens have succeeded in this challenge, make it more difficult by having them use one hand only, or index fingers only. In this activity, everyone must work together to make success a reality for anyone.
- Invite participants to line up in birthday order—without talking about their birthdates. The challenge of communicating nonverbally may be new for many tweens, who also may be surprised at how quickly they adapt. After the activity, talk about what worked, what was most difficult, and what participants noticed about one another or about the challenge. Group dynamics

may change as nonverbal communication comes into play, particularly during this game which requires participation from everyone. Tweens may notice that there were multiple ways to communicate birthdays, and all of the ways were effective, leading to a discussion about differences, similarities, and assumptions about right and wrong strategies.

TEEN PROGRAMS

Writers and Artists Celebrate Equality

Host these programs as separate one-time events, or structure them as an ongoing, multipart book club. Play up the writing and art themes of these titles, which lend themselves to related hands-on activities.

Dear Martin by Nic Stone follows Justyce, an African American high schooler, who attends a private school but grapples with his identity there, particularly through friendships and romantic relationships. An incident involving a white police officer makes Justyce examine injustices and what it means to be a black male teenager in America. Throughout the book, Justyce explores the legacy of Dr. Martin Luther King Jr., keeping a journal of reflections in the form of letters to the late civil rights leader. To complement a discussion of this book, guide teens in creating their own journals. A Beautiful Mess has posted step-by-step instructions for making journals; many other ideas and patterns are available online.[4]

Genesis Begins Again by Alicia D. Williams features a main character who makes a long list of things she hates about herself and her family. There are so many things she wishes she could change. Only when she begins noticing things that she does like about herself does she begin to understand her real power and potential. Follow a discussion of this book with a list-making activity. Try these ideas:

- Provide a variety of paper and writing utensils, and invite teens to create individual lists of their choosing (such as "Things I Love about the Library").
- Hang sheets of butcher paper on the walls, and give each one a heading (or better yet, invite teens to choose and write the headings), then set participants free with markers to add to the lists.
- Along with paper and pens, provide rulers and other art supplies, such as stickers, glitter, and rubber stamps, and invite teens to create their own lined paper—perfect for making lists at home.

The March series by John Lewis and Andrew Aydin is a trio of autobiographical graphic novels about the civil rights movement, told from the perspective of former Congressman John Lewis. Using these books as a springboard, invite teens to illustrate equality in comic form. Provide comic strip-style templates, such as the free printables from Canva, and writing and drawing utensils.[5] Encourage participants to fill in the spaces with stories—autobiographical, biographical, or fictional—showing issues of justice and equality.

The Night Diary by Veera Hiranandani is set in 1947, just after the separation of Pakistan and India. Nisha's family become refugees, traveling from Pakistan to India in search of safety. Told in the form of letters to her late mother, written in Nisha's special diary, this story brings to light a tumultuous time in history and the difficulty of trying to find a place that feels like home. After discussing this book, invite participants to create cards or stationery and write letters. If writing letters isn't a good fit for your group, consider having teens make sets of cards and packaging them with a ribbon, charm, or other embellishment. These could be sent home or sold as part of a Friends of the Library book sale or fundraiser.

Starfish by Lisa Fipps tells the story of Ellie, who has been fat-shamed for most of her life. In an effort to become as low-profile as possible, Ellie comes up with the Fat Girl Rules, a series of guidelines (such as "Don't eat in public") that she hopes will help her avoid scrutiny. Thanks to her support system, Ellie begins to accept herself for who she is, and she starts to rewrite the Fat Girl Rules. After or during your discussion, make Affirmation Rocks. Provide flat, palm-sized stones and acrylic paint (paint pens work well for this). Invite teens to write short, uplifting words or phrases, such as "You're beautiful the way you are" or "You are important." Encourage participants to place their rocks around the library or neighborhood, where others might come across them unexpectedly.

PASSIVE PROGRAMS

Art Wall

In *Hey, Wall* by Susan Verde, a boy makes a big change to the wall in his community, sparking a community art project. Display this book and others involving art, walls, and community near your passive programming space. Create an art wall by hanging butcher paper and providing a variety of art supplies. Invite library visitors to decorate the wall with pictures and positive messages.

Civil Rights Trivia

Create a quiz for patrons to take any time they're at the library. Type all of your questions on one page, and set copies at your passive programming station, or post questions on the wall and have library visitors submit answers via sticky note. Include questions such as:

- Where did Martin Luther King Jr. deliver his famous "I Have a Dream" speech? (The Lincoln Memorial, Washington, DC)
- Which state was the first to grant women the right to vote? Bonus question: What year did this take place? (Wyoming, 1890)
- In what year was segregation in public schools prohibited by the U.S. Supreme Court decision *Brown vs. Board of Education*? (1954)
- In what year was the Americans with Disabilities Act signed into law, protecting individuals with disabilities from discrimination? (1990)

Check It Out!

Create a display of books, DVDs, and recorded music reflecting diverse cultures. Encourage patrons to check these out—and even find their favorites in the collection to add to the display.

Connections

Cut construction paper in various colors into long rectangles, approximately one and a half inches wide. Set out crayons, pens, and markers, and post the prompt, "What makes you you?" Encourage library visitors to choose a paper rectangle and write one or more characteristics about themselves. These could include favorite foods, family structure, place of origin, vocation, or any other elements. Ask patrons to return the completed rectangles to the circulation or reference desk; as rectangles are returned, add them to an ever-growing paper chain in a highly visible part of the library.

COMMUNITY CONNECTIONS

- Create a "This Is Who We Are" podcast. Interview community members, asking them about their lives and backgrounds. Consider also interviewing a local civics professor, who could talk about equality issues in your specific community.

- Host a series of musicians, highlighting songs and dances from around the world. If possible, build in time for audience members to try singing along or dancing a few steps. Display books reflecting each region, and consider providing snacks that are from these areas as well.

NOTES

1. United Nations, Department of Economic and Social Affairs, Sustainable Development, "Goals, 10," https://sdgs.un.org/goals/goal10.
2. Griffin Museum of Science and Industry, Science at Home, "Egg Drop Challenge," www.msichicago.org/science-at-home/hands-on-science/egg-drop-challenge.
3. Science4Us, "Back-to-School Science Activity," https://science4us.explorelearning.com/elementary-science-projects/back-to-school-science-activity.
4. A Beautiful Mess, "Gift Idea: Homemade Journals," March 24, 2017, https://abeautifulmess.com/gift-idea-homemade-journals/.
5. Canva, "Comic Strip Templates," www.canva.com/comic-strips/templates/.

11 Sustainable Cities and Communities

Sustainable development goal 11: Make cities and human settlements inclusive, safe, resilient and sustainable.[1]

THIS SUSTAINABLE DEVELOPMENT goal focuses on the places where people live. Currently, billions of people around the world live in slums, air pollution is an increasing issue, and many individuals and families have limited or no access to public transportation or all-weather roads. This goal aims to increase public spaces, access to safe, reliable, and sustainable transportation, and safe housing.[2] Explore this goal through books and activities centered on homes, neighborhoods, and cities.

FAMILY PROGRAMS

Strong Foundations

Share any version of *The Three Little Pigs* (or make up your own version, with the help of participants). Families with school-aged children may enjoy *The True Story of the Three Little Pigs* by Jon Scieszka, or *The Three Little Pigs: An Architectural Tale* by Steven Guarnaccia. Provide art and building supplies of your choice and invite families to choose materials and build structures mimicking the little pigs' houses. Alternatively, pre-pack boxes with building supplies, and have each family choose one box without looking inside.

Additional optional challenges include requiring structures to accommodate a small toy pig (or three), requiring a specific height or width, or the structure being strong enough to hold up to the wind created by a fan or bellows.

Fort Fest

Book talk or read aloud fort-related books, such as *The Fort* by Gordon Korman, *The Little Red Fort* by Brenda Maier, and *The Fort* by Laura Perdew. Provide (or ask participants to bring) blankets, yoga mats, and other fort-building materials. Large clamps, often found at hardware stores, can be helpful, as can lengths of PVC pipe and connectors. Flashlights add a special touch. Invite patrons to build blanket forts; depending on your space, this may be one large communal fort or multiple smaller forts. Be sure to have plenty of books on hand for families to read inside the finished product.

Messages All Around

In a city, we're often bombarded with messages: advertisements, informational signs, street signs, place names, and more. At the same time, we send messages to others in our community through our expressions, actions, and words—both spoken and written. Celebrate the creation and sending of messages in a community with books such as *I Wrote You a Note* by Lizi Boyd and *Between Two Windows* by Keisha Morris. Invite participants to write notes to specific people or messages of kindness and affirmation that could be appreciated by anyone. Provide paper, writing supplies, and envelopes (for an added element, teach families how to make envelopes). Consider bringing along string and clothespins to set up a message system like the one in *Between Two Windows*. If you like, collect the messages that could be intended for anyone and use them in the "Deliver the Letter" passive program described later in this chapter.

Our Home

Share home-related books, such as *Home Is in Between* by Mitali Perkins, *Home* by Carson Ellis, *Our Home* by Lori Sugarman-Li, *A Place Called Home* by Kate Baker, *If You Lived Here* by Giles Laroche, and *Everybody in the Red Brick Building* by Anne Wynter. Ask families to share words that describe their homes. Even though homes can take many different forms, they can often be described with similar words, such as "happy," "full," "busy," or "familiar." Invite families to create pieces of décor for their homes. Choose any project you like; consider yarn wreaths, garlands made with paper, beads, or other materials, picture frames, handprint art, or some other project (check your collection for books full of ideas for kid-friendly home décor projects).

TWEEN PROGRAMS

Up on the Roof

Discuss or book talk *Rooftoppers* by Katherine Rundell, which follows twelve-year-old Sophie, who, as a baby, was found floating in a cello case after a shipwreck. She has lived happily with her (male) guardian since then, but London in the 1890s doesn't approve of the situation, and Sophie is slated to move into an orphanage. Desperate to believe that her mother is still alive, and just as desperate to locate her, Sophie and her guardian set off on a quest to Paris with the last remaining shred of identification that may lead them to their goal. Much of the story is spent on the rooftops of Paris; expand on the rooftop theme with a hands-on activity. Provide clear, open-topped rectangular containers (such as small storage bins or organizational bins meant for a refrigerator), along with a variety of art and building supplies. Ahead of time, cut colorful construction paper rectangles to fit the bottoms of the containers, and place them inside prior to the program. Challenge small groups to work together to build roofs that cover the containers' openings. Test the roofs against water; spray from a consistent distance, counting the number of sprays until you begin to see water falling on the construction paper inside a container. Repeat with all roofs, and determine which required the largest number of sprays before taking in water. Talk about the designs and their characteristics.

In the Garden

Me and Marvin Gardens by Amy Sarig King tells the story of Obe, whose family's farmland has been sold to developers. As Obe is hanging out in the last remaining wild patch, he witnesses a strange creature eating plastic. Marvin Gardens (the mysterious animal) and Obe become close, and Obe must determine how to protect his new friend. After discussing or book talking this title, talk about the concept of introducing buildings into previously undeveloped areas, and about plastic as a product and a threat to the environment. Next, set participants up with clipboards, paper, and writing utensils, and send them on a mission around the library to locate and list as many items as possible that are made of plastic. When tweens return with their lists, compile them into one large list, titled "Menu for Marvin Gardens." The number of plastic items, and the ease with which they are found, may be surprising.

My Place

Discuss or book talk Renee Watson's *Some Places More Than Others*, about Amara, whose greatest desire is to visit her extended family in New York City. But when her wish comes true, the city isn't what she had imagined. The subway is confusing, and people are everywhere. Disappointed and frustrated, Amara continues to explore and inquire, seeking a connection to her family, which she ultimately finds. As a group, talk about Amara's experience imagining the perfect place to visit—and then being disappointed. Have tweens work in small groups to create advertisements for perfect places. First, they'll have to decide which characteristics a "perfect" place has, and then they'll need to choose an advertisement format. Written ads, illustrated ads, even audio or video ads are all possibilities. When the groups are finished, ask them to share their advertisements with one another.

Shelter and Sunshine

Book talk or discuss *Shelter* by Christie Matheson. Tragedy befalls fifth-grader Maya's family, and suddenly she's dealing with homelessness, along with bullying, surviving a rainstorm with nothing to protect her, and traveling by herself all the way across the city. No matter what, though, Maya holds onto hope that the sun will shine again. To accompany this book, invite tweens to create proverbial sunshine by writing uplifting or affirming notes, possibly even on paper they have decorated with a sunshine theme. Offer the option to write a note to a specific person and take it home, or to write a note that anyone could enjoy, and add it to the "Deliver the Letter" passive program outlined later in this chapter. Alternatively, or in addition, take inspiration from Maya's cross-city venture, and play a game in pairs. Designate a starting zone, where everyone begins. Provide a variety of small stuffed animals, and ask each team to choose one to be its mascot. Collect the mascots, and have one person from each team close their eyes or put on a blindfold. Scatter the mascots around your program space. Non-blindfolded players remain in the starting area, giving their teammates instructions on how and where to move their bodies in order to find their team's mascot. Once every team has succeeded, switch player roles and play again.

TEEN PROGRAMS

Host a multipart book club, offering a discussion of one book and a related activity at each meeting, or select one or more of the following as stand-alone programs.

There Goes the Neighborhood

Discuss *There Goes the Neighborhood* by Jade Adia, a story about Rhea and her friends who find themselves in over their heads after attempting to protect their beloved and quickly gentrifying South L.A. neighborhood. In this book, the main character attempts to create an illusion of gang violence to scare off developers. Look to your nonfiction magic collection for illusions to teach participants. Try these together; they may provide a needed shift to lightheartedness after the book's heavy topics.

Facing the Sun

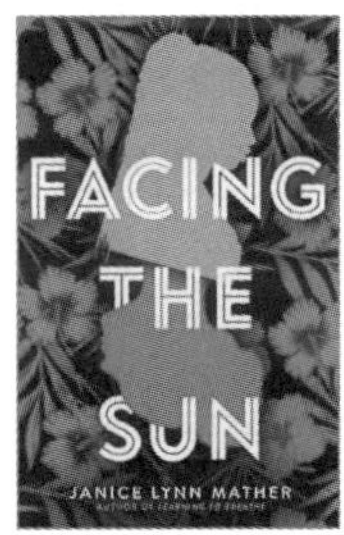

Janice Lynn Mather's *Facing the Sun* gives an intimate look into the lives of four friends whose local Bahaman beach has been purchased by a hotel developer. Readers will become invested in each character's personal story as they discover what the purchase of the beach means to the community. Follow the discussion with beach-inspired games, such as Frisbee, ladder ball, or volleyball.

Darius the Great Is Not Okay

Host a discussion about the novel *Darius the Great Is Not Okay* by Adib Khorram, about a Portland teenager who has never really felt that he fits in at home. Now he's going to Iran for the first time, and he's wondering if he'll feel the same way there, despite being half-Persian. Readers will experience life in the city of Yazd. The buildings, the culture, and the language are all new to Darius, but with unexpected help from a new friend, he may end up feeling more at home than he ever has. In the book, Darius works at a tea shop, selling teas with what he considers to be ridiculous names. Use this as inspiration for a tea tasting. Prepare a variety of teas, and have teens taste one at a time, attempting to identify the flavors. Alternatively (or in addition), invite participants to come up with original names for tea flavors. If you like, give awards for the silliest, most delicious-sounding, longest, and grossest-sounding flavor names.

The Hate U Give

Angie Thomas's *The Hate U Give* introduces sixteen-year-old Starr, who lives in a poor neighborhood and goes to school in a wealthy suburb. The stark difference between the two communities has always felt uncomfortable to Starr. When she witnesses her unarmed friend's fatal shooting by a police officer, that discomfort explodes as she weighs the potential ramifications of her testimony. This is the first in a series of books; consider following the discussion with book talks and sneak peeks at the rest of the series, or show the film version of *The Hate U Give*.

PASSIVE PROGRAMS

Paper City

Stock your passive programming station with paper in a variety of colors and patterns (withdrawn magazines and paper, such as construction paper and scrapbooking paper, left over from previous programs work well), along with scissors, markers, and any other art supplies you choose. Invite library visitors to create two-dimensional buildings by cutting and decorating paper of their choice. Encourage participants to add details, such as people, animals, windows, and doors, and to label the building with its intended purpose (for example, Department Store, Library, Office, Apartments, or Grocery Store). Ask patrons to submit their finished buildings at the circulation or reference desk, and have a staff member add them to a growing display. To create the display, simply attach the buildings at the base of a wall or large sheet of cardboard. If you like, invite patrons to submit ideas for the paper city's name, and hold a drawing or an online vote to select one.

Deliver the Letter

Set up a message delivery system using string and clothespins, such as the ones used in the book *Between Two Windows*, in which two girls send notes to each other by attaching notes onto a clothesline using clothespins. If you like, on the string, clip pre-written messages from your family or tween program, or messages that have been written by staff or volunteers. Set out paper and writing supplies, and invite library visitors to send messages to one another.

Scrambled Cities

Post trivia related to cities on a wall or bulletin board, or create a handout for patrons to complete at the library or at home. Scramble the letters of the city's name, and challenge participants to unscramble the letters to come up with the city's name. Try the following trivia to get you started:

- In 1962, Tokyo was the first city in the world to reach a population of over 10 million people.
- The "Pizza Principle" (the idea that the price of a slice of pizza matches the price of a public transit ride) was established in New York, in 1980—and still holds true today.
- Nouakchott is the capital city of Mauritania.
- Istanbul is located in two continents at once.

At Home with Literary Characters

Test patrons' knowledge with a matching game. Create one column of homes and another column of book characters. Ask participants to match the character with the corresponding home. Consider including the following:

- Villa Villekulla (Pippi Longstocking)
- The Plaza Hotel (Eloise)
- A nut tree (Scaredy Squirrel)
- A red doghouse (Snoopy)
- A hobbit-hole (Bilbo Baggins)
- An underwater kingdom (Ariel)

COMMUNITY CONNECTIONS

- Feature guest speakers such as architects, city planners, and engineers. Your municipality likely has staff members who specialize in the planning and building of cities.
- Connect with local groups that library patrons may wish to support through volunteerism. These may be groups focused on cleaning up parks, planting flowers in public spaces, shoveling sidewalks in the winter and mowing lawns in the summer for individuals who need assistance, and more. Post information on a bulletin board, or hold a community resource volunteer fair where patrons can connect with volunteer groups.

NOTES

1. United Nations, Department of Economic and Social Affairs, Sustainable Development, "Goals, 11," https://sdgs.un.org/goals/goal11.
2. United Nations, *The Sustainable Development Goals Report 2023: Special Edition* (United Nations, 2023), https://unstats.un.org/sdgs/report/2023/.

12 Responsible Consumption and Production

Sustainable development goal 12: Ensure sustainable consumption and production patterns.[1]

EVERYTHING WE USE each day—including the food we eat, the water we use, the clothes we wear, the homes we live in, the technology we depend on, and the vehicles that get us from place to place—has an environmental impact. Of course, the impact can vary from minimal to extreme. Currently, humans are consuming resources at a faster rate than the planet can support. This sustainable development goal focuses on responsible use of resources in the way items and services are created, and in the way they're used. Food waste solutions, recycling, repurposing, and owning less are all related to SDG 12. Empower library patrons to incorporate this goal with programming centered on the responsible use of resources in our daily lives.

FAMILY PROGRAMS

Trade It!

Host a book, clothing, or toy swap event; invite participants to bring items they're no longer using, set them on tables, and then browse the tables to find items they would like to take home. Anything remaining at the end of your program can be donated to a local secondhand shop.

Trash to Treasure

Share a book such as *Magic Trash: A Story of Tyree Guyton and His Art* by J. H. Shapiro, *One Plastic Bag: Isatou Ceesay and the Recycling Women of the Gambia* by Miranda Paul, or DK's *Recycle and Remake: Creative Projects for Eco Kids*. Provide materials for your choice of eco-friendly projects; if families need to bring any supplies, let them know when they register, and be sure to include this in your advertising.

Stitched Together

Ahead of time, procure enough fabric (this could be in the form of garments), either through thrift store purchases or donations, to cut one six-inch square per family or participant. At the program, guide families through choosing their fabric, measuring, and cutting the squares. Invite them to embellish their squares with paint, sewn-on buttons, permanent markers, or other items. Collect all of the squares and, after the program, sew them together into a quilt top. If you like, add batting and a back. Hang the finished product in the library so that all visitors can enjoy this community artwork.

Too Much Stuff!

The more stuff we own, the greater our strain on the environment. Share the book *Too Much Stuff!* by Emily Gravett, all about a pair of magpies who are building a nest. They start with the basics (mud, sticks, and grass) but soon get carried away, adding anything and everything to their structure. After the book, play a large group game called Birds' Nest. Set five hula hoops ("nests") on the ground in your program space (or outdoors, if possible) and place four of the hoops spread out in a square formation, with the fifth hoop in the center. Add at least twenty-four bean bags to the center hoop; the bean bags represent eggs. Divide your group into four teams, and have each team line up at one of the four corner nests. When the game begins, one player from each team runs to the center nest, picks up an egg, and returns it to their team's nest. Then the next player from each team runs in to collect an egg. Continue until one team has six eggs; this is the winning team. Make this into a cooperative game by setting up just one empty nest and spreading the eggs all around the program space. Challenge the entire group to collect all of the eggs. Use a stopwatch to determine the time it takes, and then redistribute the eggs and try again for a shorter time.

TWEEN PROGRAMS

A Good Yarn

Organize a tween knitting or crochet club, led by a staff member or community volunteer who is comfortable teaching beginners. In your library newsletter, ask for donations of yarn and needles, or visit a secondhand store for these supplies. Take your supply gathering to the next level by finding a cast-off sweater that can be unraveled and used for yarn-based projects (this can be tricky, but it's also very gratifying, and tweens will love helping unravel the sweater).

Reuse-It Challenge

Host an energy-filled program focused on the creative reuse of items. Provide a variety of items, such as plastic bottles (empty and clean), cardboard boxes, plastic bags, and withdrawn library books. Give tweens a few items and a specific amount of time (try starting with five minutes) to work in small groups to determine how to reuse the items. Encourage participants to get creative and think of practical creations. If you wish to use the items again, ask tweens to simply explain what they have in mind; if you have plenty of materials and don't need to preserve them, invite attendees to actually create the item they've imagined. Have tweens share with the large group about what they've created or designed. If you like, continue this activity by mixing up group participants, handing out new materials, and shortening the work time. Discuss or book talk *The Outcasts of 19 Schuyler Place* by E. L. Konigsburg, in which main character Margaret must help protect the works of art her uncles make out of scraps of metal, glass, and porcelain; or *The Seventh Most Important Thing* by Shelley Pearsall, the story of Arthur, who (unwillingly) finds himself indebted to the Junk Man, who sifts through trash and collects trash in his old shopping cart, for 120 hours of community service.

Color Me Responsible: Melted Crayon Pendants

Give old crayons a new life! You'll need:

- Crayons, with the labels peeled off (tweens can help with this)
- Clean, dry plastic caps from bottles or jugs
- A very small drill
- Eye screws just slightly larger than the drill bit
- Fast-drying glue
- Cord or string
- Heat guns
- Cheese graters
- Plates (paper or other, depending on the availability of dish-washing facilities; withdrawn books would work in place of plates if you prefer)
- Dimensional adhesive, such as Glossy Accents (optional)

Select crayons in any color combination (two or three colors work well). Grate them to create small piles of each color. Place the lid or cap, open-side up, on the plate. Add the crayon shavings to the cap. The shavings should be piled high, as they shrink down throughout the process. Once the shavings are in the cap, use a heat gun to melt the shavings, leaving the cap on the plate for easy clean-up. Allow them to cool, then drill a small hole in the side of the cap (this will be the top of the pendant). Add an eye screw to the hole, and attach a cord or string to make a necklace. If you like, seal the wax with dimensional adhesive, which will need to dry at least overnight before being touched.

Spread the Word on Food Waste

Approximately 30–40 percent of the food in the United States is wasted.[2] Not only are we throwing away food that could be used to feed hungry people; we're also wasting the energy and resources that go into growing, producing, and transporting that food. And then there's the issue of what to do with the food; much of it ends up in landfills. Provide QR codes that lead to websites that include food waste information, and invite tweens to follow the codes and peruse the sites, sharing interesting data as they find it. A few sites to try:

- USDA Food Waste FAQs[3]
- World Wildlife Fund: Be a Food Waste Warrior[4]
- McKinsey for Kids: (Food) Waste Not, Want Not[5]

Together, create posters, a short article for the library newsletter, or even video messages that can be posted on the library's website or social media pages, talking about the problem of food waste and positive steps we can take to help.

TEEN PROGRAMS

Sustainability Fashion Show

Invite teens to work in small groups to create wearable items made of objects that would otherwise be discarded: withdrawn books, empty (clean!) food containers, junk mail, single-use bags, and the like. When their creations are complete, set up a runway and have participants show off their creations.

Keychain This!

Give small plastic toys, which often end up in the dumpster, a new life. Ahead of time, solicit toys from the community via the library newsletter and social media pages. During the program, provide miniature hand drills and key chain parts; teach teens how to drill a small hole in the toy and add the key chain pieces, resulting in a fun, unique item to hang on a backpack. For inspiration, look online for the Little Free Keychain Library in Portland, Oregon.

Visible Mending

Invite teens to bring clothing that has holes or small tears in the fabric. Bring books, such as *Modern Mending: How to Minimize Waste and Maximize Style* by Erin Lewis-Fitzgerald and *Creative Mending: Beautiful Darning, Patching and Stitching Techniques* by Hikaru Noguchi. Provide materials such as embroidery floss, thread, needles, and fabric for patching. If a sewing expert is available in your area, invite them to assist and advise.

Local Foods Chef Challenge

The further food needs to travel, the more damage is done to the environment. With teens, research foods that are grown or made locally. A farmer, grocer, or farmers' market coordinator may be available to attend and provide insight into local foods and what the term "local" means in this context. Invite teens to create recipes or menus that include as many locally sourced items as possible. If resources and facilities allow, provide local foods for sampling or even for teens to try cooking with.

PASSIVE PROGRAMS

Pass It On

Embrace the idea of using secondhand items by setting up an ongoing swap. Focus on one type of item, such as books, snacks, or toys, or invite patrons to bring anything they'd like. The shelf for the secondhand items is available during the library's open hours, and library visitors may give or take from the shelf as they see fit. You may need to monitor the shelf or have patrons bring their items to the circulation or reference desk before adding them to the shelf, but you'll probably be surprised at the variety of items that are donated and the popularity of even the obscure ones.

Lots of Little Things

Create a community mosaic with items from patrons' homes. Invite library visitors to bring small items that are no longer serviceable—a broken toy, a single chopstick, or a cap without a bottle, for example. Be sure to specify that the items must have no sharp or jagged edges. At the passive programming station, set up a large clear container, such as a plastic jar, for patrons to place items in when they visit the library. Once the time frame for donations has ended, arrange all the items inside a large secondhand frame. Use glue or a thin set mortar to secure the objects in place. After the glue or mortar is dry, you may choose to add grout between the objects. Display this community work of art in the library.

We Reduce and Reuse

On butcher paper or a paper-covered bulletin board, post a prompt such as "I reduce my consumption of goods by . . ." or "I reuse items to help the Earth by . . ." Place pens or other writing utensils nearby, and invite library visitors to write or draw examples of their reusing and reducing efforts.

SDG 12 Fact Quiz

Create a quiz focused on this chapter's sustainable development goal. Questions might include:

- What percentage of the world's population lives in the United States and European Union, combined? (approximately 10 percent)[6]
- What percentage of the world's private consumption takes place in the United States and western Europe? (approximately 38 percent)[7]
- In the United States, what percentage of total emissions are attributed to the highest earning 10 percent of households? (40 percent)[8]
- What percentage of global greenhouse gas emissions comes from electricity and heat production? (34 percent)[9]
- What two countries in the world are responsible for the most greenhouse gas emissions? (China and the United States)[10]

COMMUNITY CONNECTIONS

- Organize an off-site visit to a recycling or water treatment facility in your area. A behind-the-scenes peek at the processes used for sanitation or recycling can be eye-opening and enthralling. If an in-person visit isn't a possibility, consider a video chat tour with a staff member at one of these facilities.
- Invite garbage collectors, a recycling coordinator from your municipality, compost specialists, and others in related fields to act as guest speakers at the library. Patrons of all ages will likely be interested to hear about their work.

NOTES

1. United Nations, Department of Economic and Social Affairs, Sustainable Development, "Goals, 12," https://sdgs.un.org/goals/goal12.
2. U.S. Department of Agriculture, "Food Waste FAQs," www.usda.gov/foodwaste/faqs.
3. U.S. Department of Agriculture, "Food Waste FAQs."

4. World Wildlife Fund, Teaching Resources, "Be a Food Waste Warrior," www.worldwildlife.org/teaching-resources/toolkits/be-a-food-waste-warrior.
5. McKinsey & Company, "McKinsey for Kids: (Food) Waste Not, Want Not," March 23, 2021, www.mckinsey.com/featured-insights/mckinsey-for-kids/food-waste-not-want-not.
6. Data based on 2022 stats from the UN, US Census, and European Union: United Nations, "Population," www.un.org/en/global-issues/population, US Census Bureau, "U.S. and World Population Clock," www.census.gov/popclock/, and Eurostat, "Demography of Europe – 2023 Edition," 2023, https://ec.europa.eu/eurostat/web/interactive-publications/demography-2023.
7. Private consumption was calculated based on two-thirds of GDP from 2023 stats from World Bank: World Bank, "GDP (current US$)," https://data.worldbank.org/indicator/NY.GDP.MKTP.CD.
8. Bella Isaacs-Thomas, "This Study Calculated the Carbon Emissions of Getting Rich," PBS News, August 29, 2023, www.pbs.org/newshour/science/this-study-calculated-the-carbon-emissions-of-getting-rich.
9. Environmental Protection Agency (EPA), "Global Greenhouse Gas Overview," last updated September 10, 2024, www.epa.gov/ghgemissions/global-greenhouse-gas-overview.
10. EPA, "Global Greenhouse Gas Overview."

13
Climate Action

Sustainable development goal 13: Take urgent action to combat climate change and its impacts.[1]

CLIMATE CHANGE IS a pressing issue that demands immediate action. Earth is getting steadily warmer and Arctic ice is melting, causing sea levels to rise. This results in lost habitats for animals and lost homes for people. Global warming also increases the risk of wildfires and weather-related disasters, such as hurricanes and drought.[2] How can young people help to fight global warming? Education is key; by learning about the issues and solutions, and by becoming comfortable talking about these topics, individuals of all ages will be empowered to make impactful changes and spread the word about climate change. The National Center for Science Education offers a basic overview of the topic of climate change; this is a great place to start gathering information.[3]

FAMILY PROGRAMS

Host an ongoing club or program, featuring books and one activity at each meeting. Alternatively, hold a larger family program, and invite participants to try all of the activities and explore a wide range of titles suggested in this chapter. Choose fiction and nonfiction books from your collection about global warming and climate change. Any of the books suggested in this chapter may fit well with your audience; a few additional suggestions including the following:

- *Glacier on the Move* by Elizabeth Rusch
- *Greta and the Giants* by Zoë Tucker
- *Iceberg: A Life in Seasons* by Claire Saxby
- *If Polar Bears Disappeared* by Lily Williams
- *Meltdown* by Anita Sanchez
- *Old Enough to Save the Planet* by Loll Kirby
- *68 Ways to Save the Planet Before Bedtime* by Paul Mason

Greenhouse Effect

Participants may be surprised to learn that the greenhouse effect is natural, normal, and essential to the functioning of our planet. The sun warms the Earth during the day, and some of that warmth remains even after daytime, having been trapped by greenhouse gases. This means that humans, plants, and animals can survive, protected from the cold we would experience without greenhouse gases and the greenhouse effect. Unfortunately, due to the unnatural quantity of greenhouse gases humans have added to the atmosphere, the greenhouse effect is more powerful than it should be, and global warming is the result.

Illustrate the greenhouse effect by placing two identical thermometers in a sunny spot. Seal one of the thermometers inside a clear glass jar, bowl, or vase. Cover the container's opening with a dark piece of cloth. Every few minutes during your program, have families check the thermometers. If you like, provide note-taking supplies to keep track of temperature readings throughout the event.

Greenhouse Gases

Greenhouse gases, such as water vapor, carbon dioxide, ozone, nitrous oxide, and methane, trap the sun's energy and also absorb heat, preventing it from leaving the atmosphere and going back into space.

Try an experiment with carbon dioxide gas, which can be produced by mixing baking soda and vinegar. You'll need four zip-close sandwich bags, a permanent marker, facial tissues, vinegar, baking soda, water, and a tablespoon measure. First, create four baking soda packets by laying a facial tissue on a table, placing two tablespoons of soda in the center, and folding carefully. If the tissues are thin, you may need to layer two together. Label each bag using numbers 1–4 (or your choice of labels; encourage families to be creative and name the bags). Fill the bags as follows:

- Bag 1: 2 tablespoons of vinegar
- Bag 2: 8 tablespoons of vinegar
- Bag 3: 12 tablespoons of vinegar
- Bag 4: 4 tablespoons of vinegar and 4 tablespoons of water

Drop a baking soda packet into each bag, sealing quickly (the tissue will delay the reaction, giving you time to close the bag). Note what happens to each bag, observing what happens when the carbon dioxide gas fills the bag and needs more space. Encourage participants to experiment with other combinations and measurements.

A more involved, related experiment is detailed online at steampowered family.com.[4]

Ice Cube Meltdown

In this experiment, a plastic bag works like the atmosphere, trapping heat. You'll need two identical glass containers, such as bowls or vases, ten ice cubes of uniform size, cold water, a clear plastic bag, a source of heat (this could be the sun or a heat lamp), and a thermometer.

In each container, place water (make sure that each one contains the same amount) and five ice cubes. Leave one container uncovered, and use the bag to cover the other. The bag represents the Earth's atmosphere. Place both containers in a warm spot. After thirty minutes, check the temperature of the water in each one. If time allows, measure the temperature again after another thirty minutes has passed.

Carbon Footprint

Provide QR codes to carbon footprint calculators, such as the one from the Nature Conservancy.[5] Encourage families to use the calculators together, discussing their own lifestyle elements that contribute to the score. After using the calculators, talk together about which topics participants were surprised to find and any changes families hope to make in order to decrease their carbon footprints.

TWEEN PROGRAMS

Climate Club Mix and Match

Hold an ongoing book club for tweens who are interested in climate change. Choose books for discussion and activities to create meeting agendas that fit your group.

- *Drawn to Change the World*, Graphic Novel Collection, 16 Youth Climate Activists, 16 Artists, by Emma Reynolds
- *Global* by Eoin Colfer
- *Haven Jacobs Saves the Planet* by Barbara Dee
- *Mission: Arctic: A Scientific Adventure to a Changing North Pole* by Katharina Weiss-Tuider
- *Palm Trees at the North Pole: The Hot Truth about Climate Change* by Marc ter Horst

- *Two Degrees* by Alan Gratz
- *What Is Climate Change?* by Gail Herman

Climate Time Lapse

Access and explore NASA's Climate Time Machine, which shows the gradual but undeniable warming of oceans, the disappearance of sea ice, and rising global temperatures, over decades.[6] If possible, project the graphics on a large screen or wall. Invite participants to share observations and questions.

Playing with Fire

Create an original board game with a global warming theme. Players might be rewarded for taking steps to benefit the environment, or perhaps the entire group attempts to slow climate change together by collecting a certain number of points or a selection of specific tokens. Undoubtedly, tweens will have lots of ideas! If your group is large, have participants work in small groups, and have the groups play one another's games.

Spread the Word

Spread the word about global warming by creating bookmarks featuring eye-catching facts, graphics, and encouraging slogans about the potential to improve the climate situation. Concrete, positive, realistic steps, such as "Remember to turn off the lights when you don't need them!" work well for bookmarks. Place the finished projects in a basket near the circulation desk, and invite patrons to choose one as they check materials out.

Five in a Row

Provide blank bingo sheets, and encourage tweens to fill in the spaces in any order with proactive steps they can take to lessen their carbon footprints. Challenge them to return their sheets to the library when they've achieved a bingo—or better yet, a blackout. For inspiration, check out the Climate Kids Bingo activity.[7]

Ice Melt

Illustrate the concept of ice melting more quickly in the water than on land with this experiment from the Science Learning Hub.[8] You'll need two containers, ice cubes, and water. Place water in one container, leaving the other container empty. Add ice cubes to each one. Watch and observe what happens.

Polar Puzzle

For a more involved hands-on activity, try the experiment "Polar Puzzle: Will Ice Melting at the North or South Poles Cause Sea Levels to Rise?" from Science Buddies.[9] Find out whether the northern ice cap's melting or the shrinking of the Antarctic ice sheet will contribute to rising sea levels. See the Science Buddies website for step-by-step instructions. National Geographic offers a similar activity.[10]

TEEN PROGRAMS

Dry and Desperate

Discuss *Dry* by Neal Schusterman and Jerrod Schusterman, set in a fictional California drought that has caused residents to live by strict rules about water usage. But when the water runs out completely, teenage Alyssa faces life-and-death decisions to help her family survive. To accompany the discussion, view short videos from PBS Learning Media about droughts and related topics.[11] Also consider creating miniature terrariums; reuse plastic bottles and add soil, plants, and water to create closed ecosystems, in which water condenses and then falls again and again. If you like, get fancy with accessories and miniatures in the terrariums!

Good News

Discuss the book *The Story of More (Adapted for Young Adults): How We Got to Climate Change and Where to Go from Here* by Hope Jahren, which is full of pertinent information. In pairs or small groups, invite teens to peruse *The Climate Optimist* by Harvard University's School of Public Health.[12] This monthly newsletter provides positive climate news in an engaging, upbeat tone. If you like, assign one or two issues of the newsletter to each group, and ask them to report back to the larger group about what they found. Additional titles to consider for this program include *How to Change Everything: The Young Human's Guide to Protecting the Planet and Each Other* by Rebecca Stefoff and Naomi Klein, and *The Twenty-One: The True Story of the Youth Who Sued the U.S. Government Over Climate Change* by Elizabeth Rusch.

As Cold as Ice

Focus on colder temperatures with James Patterson's *The Final Warning: A Maximum Ride Novel*. In this book, Max and the rest of the Flock (six teenagers who have the ability to fly) are asked to help scientists study global warming in Antarctica. Even there, though, Max can't escape danger. Challenge teens to an Arctic vs. Antarctic quiz. Questions might include:

- From which language does the word "Arctic" come? (Greek)
- Do polar bears live in the Antarctic? (no)
- Which is larger: Australia or Antarctica (Antarctica; it is about twice the size of Australia)

Fly High

Discuss *Wings in the Wild* by Margarita Engle, a novel in verse following two teens—one Cuban refugee, one Cuban American—who meet in Costa Rica and discover that they share a passion for art, and for the environment. Teens will be enchanted by the characters' love story and their determination to fight for what is right. Offer a bird-oriented project to accompany this discussion; fold origami birds, make pom-pom birds (find instructions from many sources online, including the *Pom Maker* blog), create bags of birdseed for gift-giving, or choose another activity that fits your group and space.[13]

PASSIVE PROGRAMS

Climate Change Quiz

Create a quiz full of questions related to global warming. Post questions (and answers, if you wish) on a bulletin board, or create a handout or electronic version. Gather questions from sources such as earthday.org, energy.gov, or NASA.[14]

Taking the Temperature

In the "Greenhouse Effect" family program outlined earlier in this chapter, two thermometers were set out in a sunny spot—with one big difference. One thermometer was enclosed, while the other wasn't. Create a passive activity by leaving the thermometers in place and adding a space for library visitors to note the date, time, and temperature being reflected on each thermometer. Consider adding a column for weather, too, so that you can look for trends on sunny and cloudy days.

What Will I Do?

Create a display of books, such as the ones suggested in this chapter and others from your collection. Post a prompt on a wall or bulletin board: "What Will You Do for the Planet?" Invite patrons to write or draw actions they plan to take to create positive change for the environment.

Greenhouse Gas Match-Up

Challenge library visitors to match these greenhouse gases with their descriptions.

- Water Vapor: Water in gas form; this greenhouse gas condenses and returns to Earth as rain and snow.
- Carbon Dioxide: Made of carbon and oxygen; comes from industrial processes that burn fossil fuels, as well as from volcanoes and living and decaying organisms.
- Methane: Made of carbon and hydrogen; raising cattle, and extracting oil and natural gas from below ground are all sources of methane.
- Ozone: In the atmosphere, this layer protects us from the sun's powerful rays.
- Nitrous Oxide: Created by bacteria in soil and the ocean.
- Chlorofluorocarbons: These do not occur in nature. They damage the ozone layer.

COMMUNITY CONNECTIONS

- Invite local experts, such as ecology professors, environmental educators, and climate change activists, to talk about climate issues and practical solutions.
- During reading incentive programs, offer a prize option for readers that will make a difference for the environment. Organizations such as the Nature Conservancy, the National Forest Foundation, and the Arbor Day Foundation offer programs that turn monetary donations into trees planted. In lieu of a purchased prize, give participants the choice to have the money that would have been spent on a prize donated to a selected organization. Be sure to advertise on social media to inform readers about the option, and to celebrate the total amount that was donated.

NOTES

1. United Nations, Department of Economic and Social Affairs, Sustainable Development, "Goals, 13," https://sdgs.un.org/goals/goal13.
2. United Nations, Sustainable Development Goals, "Goal 13: Climate Action," www.un.org/sustainabledevelopment/sdgbookclub-13-archive/.
3. National Center for Science Education, "Climate Change 101," January 15, 2016, https://ncse.ngo/climate-change-101.
4. Steam Powered Family, "The Greenhouse Effect Experiment," July 12, 2023, www.steampoweredfamily.com/the-greenhouse-effect-experiment/.
5. The Nature Conservancy, "How to Help: Calculate Your Carbon Footprint," www.nature.org/en-us/get-involved/how-to-help/carbon-footprint-calculator/.
6. NASA Climate Kids, "The Climate Time Machine," https://climatekids.nasa.gov/time-machine/.
7. Climate Kids, "Resources," www.climatekids.org/resources.
8. Science Learning Hub, "Melting Glacial Ice," www.sciencelearn.org.nz/resources/2279-melting-glacial-ice.
9. Science Buddies, Science Projects, "Polar Puzzle: Will Ice Melting at the North or South Poles Cause Sea Levels to Rise?" www.sciencebuddies.org/science-fair-projects/project-ideas/OceanSci_p015/ocean-sciences/will-ice-melting-at-poles-cause-sea-levels-to-rise.
10. *National Geographic Education* blog, "Weekly Warm-Up: Visualizing Climate Change," March 15, 2016, https://blog.education.nationalgeographic.org/2016/05/15/weekly-warm-up-visualizing-climate-change/.
11. PBS Learning Media for Teachers, "Climate Change Impacts and Solutions: Drought," https://pbslearningmedia.org/collection/climate-change-impacts-and-solutions/.
12. Harvard University, T.H. Chan School of Public Health, "The Climate Optimist," www.hsph.harvard.edu/c-change/climateoptimist/.
13. Pom Maker, Pom Maker Tutorial, "How to Make a Pom Pom Love Bird," https://blog.pommaker.com/how-to-make-a-pom-pom-love-bird-valentines-day-craft/.
14. Earthday.org, "Climate Change Quiz," www.earthday.org/the-climate-change-quiz/; Energy.gov, "Quiz: How Much Do You Know about Climate Change?" www.energy.gov/quiz-how-much-do-you-know-about-climate-change; NASA, "Warm Up," https://climate.nasa.gov/quizzes/global-temp-quiz/.

14
Life Below Water

Sustainable development goal 14: Conserve and sustainably use the oceans, seas and marine resources for sustainable development.[1]

THE OCEAN COMPRISES the world's largest ecosystem, and it's at extreme risk. Aside from being home to many plants and animals, the ocean provides water, food, and weather regulation. At least half of the Earth's oxygen is produced—and about a third of human-produced carbon dioxide is absorbed—by the ocean. Acid levels, plastic pollution, rising water temperatures and sea levels, and overfishing are some of the main issues facing ocean health.[2] Whether we live near an ocean or not, we're affected by the well-being of these huge but finite bodies of water. Explore and celebrate life below water with books and activities related to sea creatures, ocean exploration, and more. World Ocean Day is celebrated yearly on June 8; consider planning some of your programming around this event. You'll find ideas, information, and inspiration on the official World Ocean Day website.[3]

FAMILY PROGRAMS

Eight Arms Are Better Than Two

Octopuses provide no shortage of intrigue. Focus on these eight-armed creatures with books such as *Inky's Amazing Escape: How a Very Smart Octopus Found His Way Home* by Sy Montgomery and *The Mysterious, Marvelous Octopus* by Paige Towler. Share a hands-on STEAM activity to explore the concept of an octopus—which has no bones—fitting through a small hole. For each family or participant, you'll need:

- One gallon-size zip-top plastic bag
- Permanent marker (optional)

- Food coloring
- Instant snow (available at larger craft stores)
- One paper plate
- Scissors
- Tablespoon measure
- Cup measure
- Wide-mouth jar, quart capacity or larger

On the outside of the bag, which represents an octopus in this activity, draw an octopus using a permanent marker (optional). Add two tablespoons of instant snow powder to the bag, along with a drop or two of food coloring. Add two cups of water to the bag, seal it tightly, and mix the contents together by squeezing the bag gently. Congratulations. Your octopus is complete! Now create an obstacle for the octopus by cutting a hole in the center of the paper plate, approximately 1.5 inches in diameter. Place the plate over the top of the wide-mouth jar. Help the octopus wriggle through the hole, slowly and carefully. This may seem impossible, but your octopus is up for the challenge. Talk together about how bodies without bones move differently from our human bodies.

It's Okay to Be Shellfish

Share books related to crabs and other shellfish, such as *Crab Cake* by Andrea Tsurumi, an engaging fiction picture book about the value of each individual's contributions to a community, *What a Shell Can Tell* by Helen Scales, and *Who Would Win? Lobster vs. Crab* by Jerry Pallotta. Challenge participants to a collaborative game inspired by the sideways walk of most types of crabs. Have participants spread out in a large, open space, and instruct them to spin slowly until you prompt them to stop. When they stop, participants will be standing facing a variety of directions. Hand an item, such as a scarf or a stuffed animal, to one person, located near a corner of the playing area. Tell the group that their job is to get the item to a person in the corner furthest from the starting point—but they can only walk sideways, and the item must be passed between at least five (or another number, depending on your group size) players before reaching the end. Encourage participants to communicate and think creatively about accomplishing the task despite the limitation of only walking sideways.

Deep Dive

Marine research and exploration is fascinating and ever-evolving. Share books such as:

- *Dive! The Story of Breathing Underwater* by Chris Gall
- *The Girl Who Built an Ocean: An Artist, an Argonaut, and the True Story of the World's First Aquarium* by Jess Keating
- *Manfish: A Story of Jacques Cousteau* by Jennifer Berne
- *Ocean Speaks: How Marie Tharp Revealed the Ocean's Biggest Secret* by Jess Keating

Ocean scientists and explorers have identified distinct horizontal zones or levels in the ocean, each of which has its own characteristics and inhabitants. Invite participants to create ocean zones in a jar using online instructions from PBS Kids.[4]

Underwater Lights

Make a splash with a bioluminescence-themed program. Share books such as *Agatha May and the Anglerfish* by Nora Morrison, *Glow: The Wild Wonders of Bioluminescence* by Jennifer N. R. Smith, and *Luminous: Living Things That Light Up the Night* by Julia Kuo. Try a hands-on activity related to glowing in the dark with the glowing oil and water experiment from Play-Learn-Grow.[5]

TWEEN PROGRAMS

Tweens may enjoy programs focused on one specific ocean animal; offer a series of stand-alone events or an ongoing book club. Choose any sea creatures that are especially interesting to tweens in your community, or try the following ones to get you started.

Whales and Dolphins

Book ideas:

- *Eight Dolphins of Katrina: A True Tale of Survival* by Janet Wyman Coleman
- *Song for a Whale* by Lynne Kelly
- *Whale Done* by Stuart Gibbs
- *A Whale of the Wild* by Rosanne Parry

Accompany your discussion with a showing of the movie *Dolphin Tale*, about a rescued bottlenose dolphin. Learn more about Winter, the dolphin whose true story inspired this movie, in the book *Winter's Tail: How One Little Dolphin Learned to Swim Again* by Juliana Hatkoff, Isabella Hatkoff, and Craig Hatkoff.

Otters

Discuss *Odder* by Katherine Applegate, a novel in verse based on the sea otter rescue and foster program at the Monterey Bay Aquarium. Follow your discussion with one or both of these activities:

- Create bookmarks featuring otter-related puns, such as "You otter be reading!" or "Look on the otter side of this bookmark!" Provide step-by-step instructions for drawing otters, in case participants would like to include illustrations on their projects.
- Just like otters use rocks as tools to access food, people use tools for all sorts of things. Pull out a bag or box of everyday items you've collected ahead of time. These could include an index card, a tennis ball, a sock, a stuffed animal, and a plastic cup. Challenge tweens, in pairs, small groups, or a large group, to select one item and list as many potential uses for it as possible. Encourage them to think outside the box!

Manatees

Manatee Summer by Evan Griffith, a multilayered novel about family, nature, and friendship, provides plenty of discussion fodder. In the book, the main character and his best friend keep Discovery Journals. These are books of the wildlife they've seen in their area. Invite program participants to create their own similar journals. Start with blank notebooks and decorate the covers, or provide loose paper (consider using paper that has been printed on one side and would have been headed for the recycling bin) and binding materials. Many binding ideas can be found online; Tried & True Teaching Tools offers a tutorial on how to bind simple books using sticks and rubber bands.[6]

Mollusks

Discuss *Junonia* by Kevin Henkes, which follows Alice as she returns to the beach cottage (named Scallop) to see her friends and celebrate her birthday, as she does every year. This year, she hopes that everything will be perfect—and that she'll finally find a rare junonia seashell. After your discussion, introduce the book *Planet Ocean: Why We All Need a Healthy Ocean* by Patricia Newman, and highlight its content on ocean acidification. Set up an experiment to see first-hand how acidification can affect shells. LSU's College of Agriculture offers an activity using everyday materials; find instructions on their website.[7] Because this experiment will continue beyond the time frame of your program, consider moving it to your passive programming station, where library visitors can observe the changes in the shells.

TEEN PROGRAMS

The Thing about Jellyfish

Host a book discussion on *The Thing about Jellyfish* by Ali Benjamin, a story about death, grief, friendship, and wonder, as Suzy sets out to prove that her best friend's drowning was caused by a rare jellyfish sting. If you plan to serve snacks, and if you have facilities for boiling water, teens may enjoy creating edible jellyfish by inserting the ends of spaghetti noodles into the ends of hot dogs cut into thirds. When these are boiled, the spaghetti becomes flexible, like jellyfish tentacles. Try a jellyfish batik project to accompany your book discussion. This wax-resist process matches well with an underwater subject. Depending on your facility and resources, you may wish to use melted wax and fabric dye, as suggested by the Art of Education University, or a glue-and-paint combination might work better for you, as detailed by The Artful Parent.[8]

Picture Less Plastic

Plan a discussion of *Plasticus Maritimus: An Invasive Species* by Ana Pego and Isabel Minhós Martins, an engaging, innovative, and informative look at the issue of plastics in the ocean. This book is likely to encourage teens to take action. Invite a representative from the local recycling center, water clean-up organization, refillery, or natural foods co-op to come and talk with teens about what they can do to decrease plastic usage and make sure that the plastics they do use are recyclable. Ask teens if they have any ideas for further efforts, such as offering reusable metal water bottles as prizes, establishing a water bottle filling station at the library, encouraging restaurant patrons to bring reusable containers for leftovers, or even starting an environmental club at the library.

Journeying Deep

Challenger Deep by Neal Shusterman is a moving novel centered around Caden Bosch, a teen who lives with schizophrenia and hallucinates a harrowing adventure into the Mariana Trench. This book involves serious themes, and teens may appreciate a lighthearted activity to accompany the discussion. Try showing some clips from films, such as *Finding Nemo* or *The Little Mermaid*—while these are made for kids, teens often love them! If your group is in the mood for something more serious, consider *20,000 Leagues Under the Sea* or *Titanic*.

Fact or Fable

Discuss *The Adventures of Amina al-Sirafi*, a historical fantasy novel by Shannon Chakraborty set on the high seas. Pirates, mysteries, sorcerers, and mythical creatures abound in this book. While the sea life in the book is fantastical, it does provide a nice bridge to talking about oceans as a backdrop for stories (and life). Accompany your discussion with a game: using nonfiction books, such as *The Strangest Thing in the Sea and Other Curious Creatures of the Deep* by Rachel Poliquin, challenge teens to give three or four facts about a sea creature—the less believable they are, the better. The rest of the group must guess the creature's identity based on the facts given. If you like, keep track of the clues and answers, and use them later at your passive programming station.

PASSIVE PROGRAMS

How It Started . . . How It's Going

Display books about the ocean's origin and residents, such as *How the Sea Came to Be: And All the Creatures in It by* Jennifer Berne, *Amazing Oceans: The Surprising World of Our Incredible Seas* by Annie Roth, and *Timelines of Nature: Discover the Secret Stories of Our Ever-Changing Natural World* by DK. If you carried out the tween "Mollusks" program, outlined earlier in this chapter, include the shell acidification experiment at the passive programming station so patrons can see acid's effect in action. Alternatively, or in addition, add more and different shells (or other objects) to the water. Invite patrons to add their observations to a notebook or a large sheet of paper posted on the wall.

Way Down Deep

Choose books that highlight marine scientists, such as *Shark Lady: The True Story of How Eugenie Clark Became the Ocean's Most Fearless Scientist* by Jess Keating, and *The Vast Wonder of the World: Biologist Ernest Everett Just* by Mélina Mangal. Give patrons a chance to carry out a science experiment of their own. Create take-home packets containing instructions and materials (aside from water and plastic bottles) for making a Cartesian diver experiment. There are many ideas online for this activity; the American Chemical Society, Steve Spangler, and Thoughtfully Sustainable are a few to reference when gathering materials and creating instructions.[9]

Guess Who?

Using the clues generated by teens in the "Fact or Fable" program, set up a guessing station for library patrons. Post clues to a sea creature's identity, and challenge visitors to guess which animal is being described. If you like, continue adding clues each day or week, or provide several answer options to increase accessibility (for example, the answer might be walrus, and you could post words and/or pictures of a walrus, a shark, and an otter).

Bigger and Bigger: Math in Sea Life

Display books about the Fibonacci sequence, particularly highlighting its connection to nature. Choose books such as *Growing Patterns: Fibonacci Numbers in Nature* by Sarah C. Campbell, *Wild Fibonacci: Nature's Secret Code Revealed* by Joy N. Hulme, *Swirl by Swirl: Spirals in Nature* by Joyce Sidman, and *The Rabbit Problem* by Emily Gravett. Provide copies of a spiral created by the "golden ratio," and challenge library visitors to incorporate the spiral into a picture of their choice. Could it be an elephant's trunk? A snail's shell? Could it be filled with a bright, geometric design? If patrons wish, they may leave their artwork and have library staff add it to the wall or bulletin board.

COMMUNITY CONNECTIONS

- Seek out individuals in your community who have strong ties to the ocean. Perhaps a professor or high school teacher, a scientist, or a veterinarian would make a great guest speaker or panel member to complement your programming for this SDG.

- If you have an aquarium in your area, consider offering admission tickets to it as prizes in a reading program, or offering passes that can be checked out by library patrons. No aquarium? No problem. Tune in to a live feed from an aquarium! These are offered by many larger aquariums; locate one in your state or region, or choose one that has an upcoming special feature, such as a new aquatic resident or a soon-to-be-born baby. Play this live feed on a monitor in the library, or on a wall or big screen in the background during a program.

NOTES

1. United Nations, Department of Economic and Social Affairs, Sustainable Development, "Goals, 14," https://sdgs.un.org/goals/goal14.
2. United Nations, *The Sustainable Development Goals Report 2023: Special Edition* (United Nations, 2023), https://unstats.un.org/sdgs/report/2023/.
3. World Ocean Day, https://worldoceanday.org.
4. PBS Kids for Parents, "Make Ocean Zones in a Jar," September 27, 2019, www.pbs.org/parents/crafts-and-experiments/make-ocean-zones-in-a-jar.
5. Growing a Jeweled Rose, "Glowing Oil & Water Experiment," www.growingajeweledrose.com/2013/09/glowing-oil-water-experiment.html?m=1.
6. Tried & True Teaching Tools, "Tried & True Bookmaking: Rubberband & Stick Book," February 3, 2019, www.triedandtrueteachingtools.com/2019/02/tried-true-bookmaking-rubberband-stick.html.
7. LSU Ag Center, "Ocean Acidification," May 5, 2020, www.lsuagcenter.com/profiles/lblack/articles/page1589561125357.
8. The Art of Education University, "A Step-by-Step Guide to Batik in the Classroom," April 5, 2016, https://theartofeducation.edu/2016/04/step-step-guide-batik/; Artful Parent, Seasonal Art for Kids, "How to Do Glue Batik with Kids," May 4, 2023, https://artfulparent.com/how-to-do-glue-batik-with-kids/.
9. American Chemical Society, Celebrating Chemistry, "Cartesian Diver," www.acs.org/content/dam/acsorg/education/resources/k-8/science-activities/solidsliquidsgases/gases/cartesian-diver-science-for-kids.pdf; Steve Spangler, Inc., Sick Science! "Cartesian Divers Experiment Guide," https://stevespangler.com/wp-content/uploads/2020/07/Cartesian-Divers-Experiment-Guide.pdf; Thoughtfully Sustainable, "How to Make a Cartesian Diver Science Project for Kids," https://thoughtfullysustainable.com/cartesian-diver/.

15
Life on Land

Sustainable development goal 15: Protect, restore and promote sustainable use of terrestrial ecosystems, sustainably manage forests, combat desertification, and halt and reverse land degradation and halt biodiversity loss.[1]

HUMANS ARE RESPONSIBLE for at least 75 percent of the changes on the Earth's surface. Deforestation, irresponsible use of farmland, and lack of respect for wildlife and habitats are all leading to major issues. When habitats shrink or disappear altogether, animals are forced to find new sources of food and shelter.[2] This SDG may be approached through programming related to animals, plants, ecosystems, and habitats, topics which are often familiar and appealing for patrons.

FAMILY PROGRAMS

We Work Together

Highlight the phenomenon of symbiotic relationships at this program. Share books such as:

- *Amazing Animal Friendships: Odd Couples in Nature* by Pavla Hanackova
- *Animal Allies: Creatures Working Together* by Ginjer L. Clarke
- *Animal Sidekicks: Amazing Stories of Symbiosis in Animals and Plants* by Macken Murphy and Neon Squid
- *A Curious Collection of Wild Companions: An Illustrated Encyclopedia of Inseparable Species* by Sami Bayly
- *Just You and Me: Remarkable Relationships in the Wild* by Jennifer Ward
- *We Are Going to Be Pals!* by Mark Teague

Play a game in which participants must rely on one another, like the animals and plants you read about. Try assigning each person in the group one or two letters of the alphabet, and then having the group collectively write a message on a large sheet of paper—but each person can only write the letters they've been assigned. Alternatively, have participants work in pairs to complete a challenge, such as grabbing a pom-pom with a pair of tongs and carrying it across the room. The catch: only one person can touch the tongs and must walk backward, and another person knows where the end point or destination is and directs the pom-pom carrier there.

Making Paper

Share books related to deforestation, such as *The Great Paper Caper* by Oliver Jeffers, *Let's Save Our Planet: Forests* by Jess French, or *Zonia's Rain Forest* by Juana Martinez-Neal. Together, recycle scraps to make handmade paper, using the instructions online from Steam Powered Family.[3]

Who Am I? Animal Edition

Provide a variety of informational books about wild animals. Encourage each family or group to choose one animal and, using the books, create a list of several clues about the animal. After the clues have been written, invite each group to share their clues, while others guess at the animal being described. Program participants might also enjoy a round of charades featuring the animals they've selected.

Make a Terrarium

Terrariums give young people (and not-so-young people) the opportunity to care for a group of plants and witness their growth and changes over time. Many instructions are available online; try the ones by NASA's Climate Kids for a straightforward, flexible project.[4]

TWEEN PROGRAMS

Consider structuring tween programs around one habitat or ecosystem. Choose books with a corresponding setting, and facilitate discussion about the unique characteristics of this type of place. These programs provide springboards for deeper exploration of animals and plants that are part of the natural world.

Radiant Rainforests

Discuss the book *The One and Only Ivan* by Katherine Applegate, about a silverback gorilla who was kept in captivity for twenty-seven years until being moved to a zoo, where he lived in a simulated African rainforest habitat. Provide informational books (and links to websites, if you choose) about the African rainforest. Challenge participants to work in groups to create an African Rainforest Alphabet, listing one (or more) animal or plants that live in this type of habitat for each letter of the alphabet. At the end of an allotted time period, ask the groups to share their alphabets. The team that has completed the most letters wins. For more rainforest-related reading, try the *Lost Rainforest* series by Eliot Schrefer.

Resilient Rivers

The graphic novel *Treasure in the Lake* by Jason Pamment follows the adventures of two friends as they explore a dry riverbed and discover a hidden city. This story involves a dam; invite participants to try building a dam of their own. Provide plastic shoeboxes or other rectangular containers, as well as a variety of items tweens can use to build dams. Consider modeling clay, craft sticks, aluminum foil, and any other supplies you have handy. Working in small groups, challenge tweens to build dams across the middle of their containers. When the dams are finished, slowly pour water into one side of each container, testing to see how much water the dams will support.

Fabulous Forests

The Girl Who Drank the Moon by Kelly Barnhill and the *Wildwood Chronicles* by Colin Meloy feature forest settings. Follow a book discussion with woodland animal origami. Provide paper for folding, as well as origami books that include instructions for creatures that fit the theme. Depending on the size of your group and the age of participants, you may wish to select a few animals ahead of time and practice folding these yourself so you're ready to answer any questions that arise.

Delightful Deserts

Choose a book with a desert setting, such as *Across the Desert* and *The Canyon's Edge*, both by Dusti Bowling, or *The Burning Maze*, the third book in Rick Riordan's *The Trials of Apollo* series (this title can be read as a stand-alone). At your program, offer a sand art activity. You'll need clear bottles or jars (glass or plastic) with lids, spoons or small scoops, and colored sand. Purchase the colored sand from art supply vendors, or make your own ahead of time or as part of the program. To make your own colored sand (which is actually salt, but the finished product looks and acts like sand), you can mix table salt with food coloring to the desired color saturation. Participants will add one color at a time to their containers, creating layers of varying colors and thicknesses.

TEEN PROGRAMS

Like tween programs, teen programs for this SDG work well when structured around one particular habitat or ecosystem.

Get Prickly in the Desert

Discuss a book with a desert setting, such as *The House of the Scorpion* by Nancy Farmer. Follow the discussion with a felt succulent art project. You'll find plenty of ideas and instructions online, such as the tutorial by Six Clever Sisters.[5] Glue the felt succulents to wooden spools, wooden blocks, or cardboard boxes, any of which look like planters and can be decorated with desert animals (fine-tipped paint pens or permanent markers work well).

Stay Cool in the Tundra

Discuss books with tundra settings, such as *The Snow Child* by Eowyn Ivey, *The Call of the Wild* by Jack London, *The End of Drum-Time* by Hanna Pylväinen, and *Never Cry Wolf* by Farley Mowat. Choose a northern lights extension activity, such as:

- Use chalk in a variety of colors to draw lines on a black sheet of construction paper. Smudge the chalk with a facial tissue for an effect that suggests northern lights.
- Create northern lights in a jar. Tear several different colors of tissue paper (including black) into strips. Use Mod Podge to cover the bottom quarter of a clear glass jar in black tissue paper, evoking the night sky. Above and slightly overlapping the black tissue, add strips of other colors, overlapping and combining as you like. Once the jar is completely covered and the Mod Podge is dry, add a battery-operated tea light candle inside the jar. Turn the lights down and enjoy the glow.

See the Forest for the Trees

Wildoak by C. C. Harrington and *The Overstory* by Richard Powers both feature forest settings. Follow a discussion of these books with an opportunity for teens to try creating something out of wood. If resources and expertise allow, offer simple woodworking projects (preferably using reclaimed wood). Another option is to create shadowboxes or other displays inside discarded wooden drawers (you may need to begin collecting these well in advance of the program). Provide paint, a variety of brushes, and repurposed items such as plastic lids and small secondhand toys. If you like, display the finished projects in the library, or send them home with participants.

Marvelous Mountains

Find a mountain setting in books such as *Into the Wild* by Jon Krakauer and *Peak* by Roland Smith. During your program, invite a local rock-climbing instructor or outdoor enthusiast (you might find one through a local outdoor store, an expedition outfitter, or a student outdoor group) to talk about mountain exploration and survival. Consider holding a library outing to a rock climbing gym nearby, or offer free climbing passes as prizes or giveaways.

PASSIVE PROGRAMS

Symbiosis Guessing Game

Create an interactive activity for library visitors using the books suggested in the "We Work Together" program earlier in this chapter. Post clues to a specific symbiotic pair of animals, such as where they live, what they do for one another, their colors, and other unique features. Post the answers in a lift-the-flap format on the wall for patrons to peek at when they're finished reading the clues and formulating their guesses. Add pictures of the symbiotic pairs being described for extra clues.

I'm Home . . . or Am I?

Each week or two, post the name of a different habitat or ecosystem on a wall or bulletin board. Add pictures and/or names of the animals and plants that live in that habitat, along with a few that do not. Challenge library visitors to identify the misplaced plants and animals. Provide a display of books about the environment in question to help with this venture.

New Sensation

Display books about animal senses, such as *When Elephants Listen with Their Feet* by Emmanuelle Grundmann, *An Immense World* by Ed Yong, and *Nose Knows* by Emmanuelle Figueras. Set up sensory challenges for patrons:

- A touch-and-feel box that allows individuals to reach in and feel an object without seeing it
- An essential oil-soaked cotton ball in the bottom of a jar (be sure to post the ingredients for allergy and sensitivity purposes)
- Audio recordings of various animal noises (QR codes work well for this)

Wonderful Wild Animals

On a wall or bulletin board, post a prompt such as "What's your favorite wild animal? Why do you love it?" Nearby, provide sticky notes and writing utensils. Encourage library visitors to add their answers. Increase visibility by posting one or two responses each day on the library's social media pages.

COMMUNITY CONNECTIONS

- Invite guest speakers such as beekeepers, gardeners, and farmers to talk about the importance of respecting the environment of animals and plants.
- Host a pet adoption event through your local animal rescue. If having adoptable pets onside isn't feasible, feature a pet of the week on your library's website and social media channels.

NOTES

1. United Nations, Department of Economic and Social Affairs Sustainable Development, "Goals, 15," https://sdgs.un.org/goals/goal15.
2. United Nations, Sustainable Development Goals, "SDG15: Life on Land Reading List," www.un.org/sustainabledevelopment/sdg15-life-on-land-reading-list/.
3. Steam Powered Family, "How to Make Paper – A Recycling Craft for Kids," December 11, 2023, www.steampoweredfamily.com/how-to-make-paper/.
4. NASA, Climate Kids, "Make a Terrarium Mini-Garden," https://climatekids.nasa.gov/mini-garden/.
5. Six Clever Sisters, "How to Make Felt Succulents {that actually look real!}," September 10, 2021, www.sixcleversisters.com/how-to-make-felt-succulents-that-actually-look-real/.

16

Peace, Justice, and Strong Institutions

Sustainable development goal 16: Promote peaceful and inclusive societies for sustainable development, provide access to justice for all and build effective, accountable and inclusive institutions at all levels.[1]

INDIVIDUALS OF ALL ages can relate to the desire to be treated fairly and live a peaceful life. Indeed, these are basic human rights. Institutions, such as law enforcement, exist to enforce rules that keep people safe, allowing them to live in peace and fairness. The focus of this SDG dovetails nicely with the International Day of Peace, established by the United Nations and celebrated each year on September 21. Consider planning your programming around this date or hosting an event to observe the International Day of Peace. Find information, inspiration, and resources, including a toolkit full of ideas, online.[2]

FAMILY PROGRAMS

Sing It!

Folk singers, such as Pete Seeger and Joan Baez, have long sung songs about peace and social justice. Share books such as *The Golden Thread: A Song for Pete Seeger* by Colin Meloy and *Make a Pretty Sound: A Story of Ella Jenkins—The First Lady of Children's Music* by Traci N. Todd, along with recorded music and related online resources. Project the lyrics on a screen or wall and play the music (recorded or using live instruments, if musicians are available), inviting all participants to sing along.

Fold It!

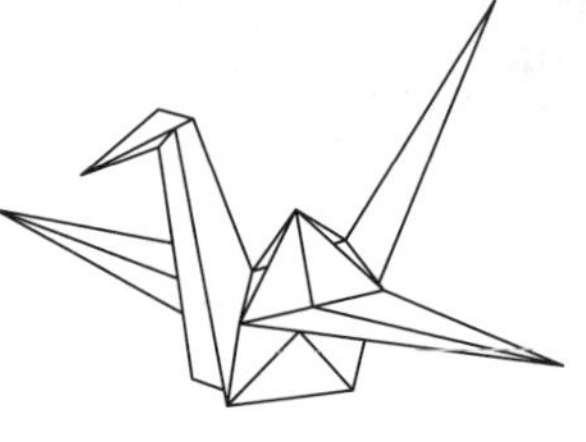

Book talk or discuss *Sadako and the Thousand Paper Cranes* by Eleanor Coerr, based on the true story of a young girl who was exposed to radiation in 1945 in Hiroshima and suffered from leukemia later in childhood. Inspired by Japanese folklore, she folded more than 1,000 paper cranes during her illness in hopes of recovery and a long life. While she passed away at age twelve, her message of peace lives on. Accompany this book talk or discussion with an origami crane workshop. Provide origami paper in a variety of sizes and styles, along with instructions and assistance. If you like, ask patrons to leave some of the cranes, and string them together to form a garland or other decoration for the library.

Take Action!

Share books about young activists for peace and justice, such as *One Peace: True Stories of Young Activists* by Janet Wilson and *Marley Dias Gets It Done and So Can You!* by Marley Dias, as well as books containing ideas for action kids can take toward peace, such as *Peace* by Miranda Paul and Baptiste Paul. Invite participants to brainstorm and share ideas for action they could take in your community. This may include raising money to contribute to a cause, bringing attention to an issue, lobbying for legislation, and more. If you like, invite representatives from area organizations that families could become involved in, such as food pantries and advocacy groups, so that patrons can connect with larger local efforts. Your group might also choose to begin a donation drive for items such as winter coats; at your program, invite participants to create signs to advertise the drive and decorate a large box or bin for donations.

Get Mindful!

Peace begins with our own bodies and minds. Feature books such as *I Am Peace: A Book of Mindfulness* by Susan Verde and *Take a Moment: 50 Mindfulness Activities for Kids* by Paul Christelis. Invite participants to try mindfulness activities, such as breathing exercises, stretching, journaling, guided meditation, and coloring. Try the Mindful Eating activity described by the Michigan State University Extension.[3]

TWEEN PROGRAMS

Noteworthy Names in Peace and Justice

Plan a multipart tween program; at each meeting, focus on a different individual who has worked for peace and justice. Invite participants to read their choice of books about the subject ahead of time. During the program, discuss what tweens read, watch online clips of the subject (if available), and try a related activity, such as:

- Craft symbols of peace, such as doves or peace symbols, using supplies such as polystyrene shrink art sheets or pages from discarded books or magazines.
- Use poster paper and art supplies to write and illustrate favorite quotes from the individual being discussed.
- Write positive messages outside the library using sidewalk chalk.
- Plan acts of kindness.
- Paint rocks with peaceful words or pictures, and place them around the library or community.

Book series such as *Who Was? The Story of Biographies*, *Ordinary People Change the World*, and *Little People, BIG DREAMS* feature many intriguing individuals who have worked for peace and justice. Consider the following individuals for the focus of your programs, or choose others.

- Martin Luther King Jr.
- Mother Teresa
- Jane Addams
- John Lewis
- Mahatma Gandhi

TEEN PROGRAMS

Jigsaw Book Club: The Holocaust

Invite teens to read a piece of historical fiction set during the Holocaust. Provide a list of suggested titles; try the lists curated by *School Library Journal*[4] and the Holocaust Museum in Houston[5] for ideas and inspiration. During the program, talk about the books that were read, and about the impressions these books made on readers. As the discussion progresses, the group will likely find similarities and common themes throughout the stories. If time permits, spend time together exploring the website of the United States Holocaust Memorial Museum, which features a wide range of resources, including online exhibitions.[6]

Nic Stone Book Club

Hold a book club centered around Nic Stone's *Dear Martin* and *Dear Justyce*, novels that deal with themes of racial discrimination, particularly in law enforcement and the juvenile justice system. Along with a discussion, consider having a guest speaker, such as a police officer, an attorney, or a youth justice advocate, visit your program to answer questions and talk about issues that came up in the books.

Just Mercy Book Discussion

Facilitate a discussion of *Just Mercy: A True Story of the Fight for Justice, Adapted for Young Adults*, a memoir by Bryan Stevenson. The Alabama-based author is a graduate of the Harvard Law School and the Harvard School of Government, and has worked tirelessly to combat bias against people of color and the poor. If you like, follow this discussion with a showing of the movie *Just Mercy*, or show a few online videos of brief interviews with the author.

Before We Were Free Book Discussion

Discuss *Before We Were Free* by Julia Alvarez, a novel about a girl living in the Dominican Republic in the 1960s, under the dictatorship there. In the story, three sisters, called The Butterflies, start a resistance movement against the dictator. Butterflies are a powerful symbol in this book. After your book discussion, offer a butterfly-related activity. Consider bringing several butterfly-themed coloring books for teens to tear pages from and color. Alternatively, gather secondhand picture frames and a few withdrawn books about butterflies. Invite teens to select illustrations from the books to put in the frames. If you like, also provide metallic pens or other supplies, so that participants can add text or other elements to their projects.

PASSIVE PROGRAMS

What Is Peace?

Post a prompt, such as "What is peace?" or "What does peace look like?" on a wall or bulletin board. Invite patrons to write or draw their responses on sticky notes and post them under the prompt.

Give Peace a Hand

Invite library visitors to trace an outline of their hand onto paper, cut it out, and add any pictures, colors, designs, or words they wish. Collect these at the circulation desk, and use them to create a large peace symbol on a wall.

Name That Peacemaker

Challenge patrons to match the name of a peacemaker with a brief description of that person. Make this activity more difficult by not offering a bank of names to choose from. Consider providing print biographies or QR codes that link to biographical websites to assist patrons in identifying the individuals. A few to include:

- Alokiir Malual: the first woman to sign a peace agreement in South Sudan
- Béatrice Epaye: Central African Republic parliamentarian who advocates for women's involvement in politics
- Maïga Adiza Mint Mohamed: first-ever woman parliamentarian of Timbuktu; works to increase women's involvement in peacemaking and politics
- Jane Addams: a Nobel Peace Prize recipient, nominated for her efforts to end World War I

Balance It

Justice is often symbolized by a balance scale. Set out such a scale, along with a variety of items for patrons to experiment with. If you like, add challenges, such as "Place one yellow block on one side of the scale. Try to balance it using only blue blocks on the other side. Is this possible?"

COMMUNITY CONNECTIONS

- Invite local activists, social justice leaders, law enforcement personnel, or others who work for peace and justice to speak individually or as part of a Peacemaker Panel.
- Create a forum for peace initiatives to be shared. This might be a bulletin board or a portion of the library's newsletter. Highlight work that is being done in the community, and include ideas for library patrons to help.

NOTES

1. United Nations, Department of Economic and Social Affairs Sustainable Development, "Goals, 16," https://sdgs.un.org/goals/goal16.
2. United Nations, International Day of Peace, 21 September, "2024 Theme: Cultivating a Culture of Peace," www.un.org/en/observances/international-day-peace.
3. Michigan State University, MSU Extension, "Teaching Kids the Art of Mindful Eating," April 20, 2016, www.canr.msu.edu/news/teaching_kids_the_art_of_mindful_eating.
4. Rachel Kamin, Chava Pinchuck, and Heidi Rabinowitz, "Age-Appropriate Middle Grade and YA Books About the Holocaust," *School Library Journal*, January 22, 2020, www.slj.com/story/Commemorate-Holocaust-Remembrance-Day-with-this-Booklist-libraries-students.
5. Holocaust Museum Houston, "25 Books About the Holocaust," https://hmh.org/about/25-books-about-holocaust/.
6. United States Holocaust Memorial Museum, www.ushmm.org.

17

Partnerships for the Goals

Sustainable development goal 17: Strengthen the means of implementation and revitalize the Global Partnership for Sustainable Development.[1]

WHEN IT COMES to making gains toward sustainability, a popular saying credited to John C. Maxwell is true: "Teamwork makes the dream work!" We absolutely must work together and join forces in order to make impactful changes. Just as all members of a sports team contribute to the team's collective success, so do concerned and proactive residents of Planet Earth. The seventeenth sustainable development goal focuses on cooperation, shared responsibility, and working together for common goals.

FAMILY PROGRAMS

Play Together

Host a family game event, featuring cooperative board games that are quick to learn. Try games such as *Outfoxed! Snail's Pace Race, My First Castle Panic, Castle Panic*, and others. Be sure to include a variety of games that will appeal to all ages. Consider also setting out building blocks or other materials that may lead to open-ended cooperative play.

Pass It Along

Have all participants join hands in a large circle. At one point in the circle, ask two individuals to unclasp their hands just long enough for you to loop a hula hoop over one of their arms. Ask them to reclasp their hands. Challenge the group to move the hula hoop around the entire circle without anyone unclasping hands. After they've completed this, ask them to try for a faster time, or add a second hoop to add to the challenge. Pair this activity with a round of charades or a book discussion; try *We Are All Connected: Caring for Each Other & the Earth* by Gabi Garcia or the *Changemakers* series by Loll Kirby.

Walk Together

Purchase or create cooperative walking boards (sometimes called "trolleys"), which are sets of two boards, each of which has several ropes attached. Teams of participants stand on the boards, each person with one foot on each board and holding onto one rope from each board. They then attempt to walk a specific distance or even try to navigate obstacles. Find instructions for making these boards, along with ideas for activities, online at Fun Doing.[2] If you like, accompany this experience with a discussion of books such as *Just Help!* by Sonia Sotomayor or chapter books with teamwork themes, like *Holes* by Louis Sachar or *11 Birthdays* by Wendy Mass.

Two Voices Are Better Than One

Invite participants to explore poetry for two or more voices. Provide books such as *Joyful Noise* and *Big Talk*, both by Paul Fleischman, and the *You Read to Me, I'll Read to You* series by Mary Ann Hoberman. Encourage patrons to read in any groups that feel comfortable. If there is interest, consider having a short showcase toward the end of the program, giving participants an opportunity to read multi-voice poetry aloud in front of the group. Alternatively, families may enjoy writing their own original poetry for more than one reader.

TWEEN PROGRAMS

Host a multipart tween program or club. At the first meeting, share *50 Things You Can Do to Save the World* by Kim Hankinson (consider having multiple copies on hand, so participants can flip through them during the discussion). Choose several items from the book that your group will carry out on the forthcoming program dates. Ideas in the book include hosting a plastic-free party and making megaphones and kites to share about climate change and other issues. At each meeting of your group, do one of the activities that was selected. Consider planning an additional activity; try one of the following.

Be Inspired

Read selections aloud from *Stories for Kids Who Want to Save the World* by Carola Benedetto and Luciana Giliento (this works well for an activity that requires participants to make things or wait for items to dry).

Be Playful

Try a tween-appealing cooperative game, such as *Forbidden Island*. This is part of a series of games; if you try one and it's popular, consider investing in the rest of the series.

Be Curious

Introduce tween-friendly library databases and other online sources for information on climate change, social justice, and other SDG-related content.

Be Observant

Look around the library together. What do you notice? Encourage participants to make observations about the ways people use the space, the items that are in the library (and what they're made of), and the interactions happening around the library. This may spark a discussion about the library as a community hub or an equalizer—or many other potential topics.

TEEN PROGRAMS

Movie Mania

Show a film with a teamwork theme, such as *Remember the Titans*, *A League of Their Own*, or any of the *Avengers* or *The Lord of the Rings* movies. If you select a movie based on a book, consider adding a book discussion to the program.

Spread the Word

Create short public service video announcements about SDG-related issues, such as climate change or social justice. If possible, provide a ring light, and involve teens in the editing process. Post the finished products on the library's social media pages.

Play a Game

Cooperative board games, such as *Ticket to Ride* or *Pandemic*, are perfect for participants who are getting to know one another. Ask a local game shop for game suggestions—they may even have a staff member who can come to the program to teach the game.

Together IRL (In Real Life)

Invite teens to prepare and present stories or activities at library programs for young children or to volunteer to help with programs for other ages. They may make some powerful connections, and they may see themselves as pieces of the community puzzle through these opportunities.

PASSIVE PROGRAMS

We Read Together

Create a community-wide reading log by inviting patrons to write the titles of books they read in a specific time period on sticky notes (one title per note) and adding them to a wall or bulletin board. Alternatively or in addition, ask patrons to submit photos of themselves reading with friends, family, or pets. Print these and display them.

Literary Match-Up

Challenge patrons to match the characters from well-known literary pairs. Create two lists of characters, dividing each pair so that one name appears on each list. Be sure that names are in a random order, not just across from their partners. Invite participants to identify the names that go together. Have them submit answers on paper, or post answers nearby using a lift-the-flap method. Consider including pairs such as:

- Charlie and Lola
- Hansel and Gretel
- The Ant and the Grasshopper
- The Lion and the Mouse
- Elephant and Piggie
- Frog and Toad
- Sherlock Holmes and Dr. Watson
- Katniss Everdeen and Peeta Mellark

Collaborative Story

Set out a notebook, pencil, and instructions inviting patrons to add a single word or sentence to a collaborative story. Staff may need to monitor the notebook to make sure that the content and language are appropriate for all ages. When the story is complete, or after a set amount of time, post the finished product on the library's social media pages.

Same and Different

This activity illustrates that each of us is unique, sharing similarities and differences with others in the community. Post a variety of characteristics, skills, or preferences on a wall or bulletin board. Invite library visitors to add dots using markers or stickers near the words or phrases that describe them. They'll likely notice that they share some traits with lots of people, and some with fewer, and that there are some items on the list that don't fit them at all.

COMMUNITY CONNECTIONS

- Invite sports coaches, company presidents, and others who oversee groups of people to talk on a panel about teamwork and fostering healthy teams.
- Create a multi-age library advisory panel. Take applications from all age groups, and focus on issues that matter to a wide variety of patrons. Consider asking for topic ideas on the panel application; this will give you an added sense of the applicant's priorities, and it will help you identify trends and issues the panel might address.

NOTES

1. United Nations, Department of Economic and Social Affairs, Sustainable Development, "Goals, 17," https://sdgs.un.org/goals/goal17.
2. Fundoing, "Trolley Obstacles (with Video)," January 17, 2018, www.fundoing.com/blog/trolley-obstacles-with-video.

CONCLUSION
Planting Seeds for Change

WHAT'S NEXT FOR sustainability programming? If your community has a special interest in one or more goal, topic, or theme, or if a specific type of program—such as a book club, passive programming, or hands-on STEAM project—was especially well received, use this insight to identify your next steps. Don't worry about being perfect or knowing every answer. Giving patrons opportunities to engage with sustainability topics is valuable in itself.

Consider creating a sustainability committee or club made up of patrons of various ages. These passionate individuals could carry out long-term projects, stay abreast of trends and developments in sustainability fields, and be on the lookout for community resources and opportunities. An added benefit is the building of community within the committee or club, as members of all ages come together to work toward common goals.

No matter what sustainability programming looks like in your library, know that every opportunity you provide for patrons to engage in this discovery and discussion makes an impact and plants a seed. Keep on promoting sustainability through library programming. Future generations will thank you!

INDEX

T